RESTAURANT

Secrets®

*Featuring a collection of recipes
and gift certificates from the best
restaurants in the area*

presented by

 **CUC INTERNATIONAL**

Cover photo by Michael A. Gallitelli

RESTAURANT Secrets®

Have you ever dined in a restaurant and tried to make the same meal at home but it was... different?
Upon asking the restaurant for the recipe, you heard... "it's a secret."
Well, not anymore...

**Welcome to "Restaurant Secrets" Collection Series, Volume I
featuring a collection of 50 treasured recipes from the best restaurants in the area.**

Since the beginning of time, a meal has been the universal activity that transcends
all languages and ethnic backgrounds. A grand meal is the canvas for celebrations of love and friendship.
A fine dining experience soothes the soul, nurtures the mind, and warms the heart.
"Restaurant Secrets" brings you the great meals from the kitchens of the best restaurants in the area,
and teaches you to cook like a chef in your own home.

Expert restaurateurs have taken great care in preparing their famous recipes, including every ingredient and
preparation step, so that you can easily experience the same extraordinary results at home.
You are cordially invited to "Test the Chef" with the enclosed gift certificates
and see how your versions compare to the pros!

Discover the wisdom of the area's best restaurateurs as you taste and enjoy their recipes in your own kitchen.
When a guest asks you, "What's your secret?" remember to tell them that it's not a secret anymore.

"Restaurant Secrets" Collection Series, Volume I...
Great for cooking at home, dining out, or giving as a gift!

Happy Cooking and Fine Dining!

Table of Contents

Restaurants

Kid Friendly

Banquet Facilities

HeartSmart Menu

Credit Cards Accepted

Valet Parking

Alcohol Served

Restaurant Secrets of Vancouver

Vancouver, the "World's Most Beautiful City," is where the sea meets the mountains, the past meets the future, and traditional European cuisine meets eclectic West Coast cooking.

Vancouver is the fourth fastest growing urban centre in North America and this growth and innovation is reflected in the restaurants and cuisine featured here in *Restaurant Secrets of Vancouver*.

The following recipes are presented by some of the finest chefs from your favourite restaurants. Bruno Marti, President of the British Columbia Culinary Arts Foundation states, "The chefs and restaurateurs have come together to support *Restaurant Secrets of Vancouver* by donating their favourite recipes in an effort to help local non-profit organizations raise much needed funds." Many of the chefs featured in *Restaurant Secrets of Vancouver* are members of the British Columbia Culinary Arts Foundation and are affiliated with the Canadian Federation of Chefs and Cooks, a national non-profit association that was formed in an effort to unite chefs and cooks across Canada in a common dedication to professional excellence. This unification is also evident in the culmination of *Restaurant Secrets of Vancouver*.

In doing this, we thank the restaurateurs of Vancouver, their chefs and staff, for their contribution toward enhancing the quality of life in our area.

Together with Bruno Marti and the British Columbia Culinary Arts Foundation, we invite all of you to try these recipes, sharpen your culinary skills by learning our "Restaurant Secrets" at home, and then enjoy a memorable dining experience at one of Vancouver's premier restaurants.

Thank you and Bon Appétit!

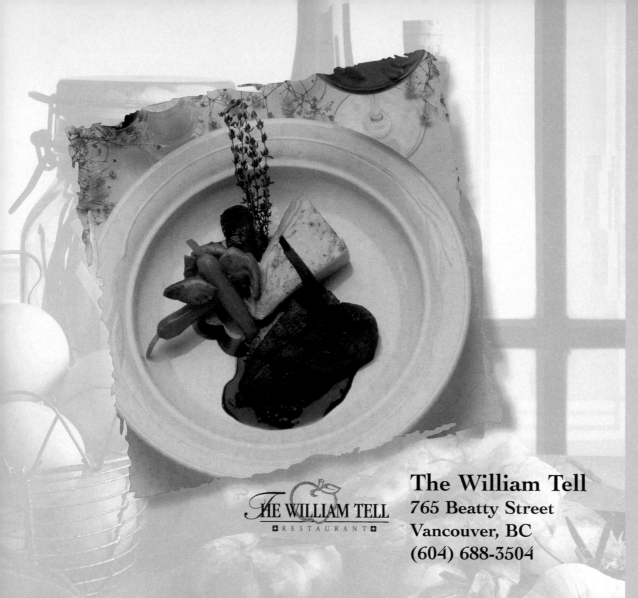

The William Tell
765 Beatty Street
Vancouver, BC
(604) 688-3504

The William Tell Restaurant has been Vancouver's favourite Swiss European restaurant for over 34 years. The combination of modern cooking and strong west coast influence — in addition to our traditional Swiss recipes — have been very well received. Executive Chef Todd Konrad and his team are constantly pushing the boundaries of inventive cuisine. For guests who are in a hurry to get to the symphony, theater, hockey or basketball game on time, the Bistro at The William Tell ensures efficient service. For private parties, there is always the Cross Bow Room — it seats up to 30 people comfortably. Valet parking is available. Visit on a Sunday night and enjoy our Swiss Farmer's Buffet. Reservations are recommended.

Roasted duck breast with leeks and Okanagan apple rosemary jus

Fraser Valley Duck Breast

Score duck and rub with cinnamon and cloves. Let stand in refrigerator while preparing terrine. Use 6 inch cast iron pan or T-fal pan. Grease with oil and layer potato slices, lining the bottom of the pan, just overlapping the edges. Repeat. Season with salt and pepper to taste. Add two pinches of leek and some cream. Continue layering in this method until all ingredients are used. Bake at 375 degrees for one hour.

To make Apple Piñot Noir Rosemary Jus, sauté shallots with oil and butter until translucent. Add apples; cook until soft, about 7 minutes. Deglaze with Piñot Noir and reduce.

Add chicken and veal stock and reduce by 1/3; season purée and add rosemary sprigs.

Over medium heat, cook breast fat side down (so fat will render itself). Cook for about 4 to 5 minutes. When browned, turn over for 1 minute to sear the meat.

Cook at 375 degrees for 7 to 8 minutes. Accompany with fresh vegetables and serve.

4 duck breasts, 6 to 7 ounces each

2 tablespoons ground cinnamon

2 pinches ground cloves

850 grams Yukon Gold potatoes, thinly sliced

50 grams leeks, finely diced

250 milliliters whipping cream

20 milliliters olive oil

20 milliliters butter, clarified

3 pieces apples, peeled, cored, diced large

50 grams shallots, peeled and sliced

salt and pepper to taste

fresh rosemary sprigs

75 milliliters Piñot Noir wine

50 milliliters chicken stock

300 milliliters veal stock

Villa del Lupo
869 Hamilton Street
Vancouver, BC
(604) 688-7436

VILLA del LUPO
RISTORANTE ITALIANO

*Villa del Lupo, or House of the Wolf—named after Romulus and Remus, the classical twins who rebuilt Rome—
has been popular with food critics and Vancouverites since opening in 1991. Chef Julio Gonzales-Perini and
General Manager Vince Piccolo have displayed a distinguished 6-year track record in the Tuscan-style villa on
Hamilton Street. Villa del Lupo has again garnered the award for Best Italian restaurant in Vancouver
Magazine's annual restaurant awards. Food critics singled out Villa del Lupo for the third consecutive year, over
at least 12 "robust Italian" contenders. Chef Julio Gonzalez-Perini was cited by one critic as "simply the best chef
in the city, with amazing technique and a love of food that is self evident." For a memorable evening of exquisite
food complemented by fine wine, visit Villa del Lupo and see why it is the ideal destination.*

Rib-eye of lamb roasted with sweet garlic, rosemary and mashed potatoes

Roasted Lamb Rib-Eye

Preheat oven to 400 degrees. Cut carrot and celery crosswise into 1/2 inch slices; dice onion. Combine vegetables with lamb bones, meat scraps, peppercorns and bay leaves in a large roasting pan. Roast in oven, stirrring occasionally until golden. Transfer to stock pot, add water and stock. Bring to a boil on medium heat and cook for 45 minutes. Strain liquid into saucepan, discard the solids. Reduce by 1 1/2 cups, correct seasonings, strain and set aside. Wash and remove tough stems from Swiss chard. Blanch in boiling salted water for 45 seconds. Drain and refresh under cold running water. Squeeze dry in a kitchen towel.

Heat 2 tablespoons oil in large ovenproof skillet on medium heat. Season lamb with rosemary, salt and pepper to taste. Place fat side down in hot pan. Sear for 3 minutes. Add garlic and sear remaining sides until just browned, turning garlic while searing lamb. Place all in preheated oven for 10 minutes until medium rare. Remove from oven and let stand for 5 minutes. Pick out garlic cloves (set them aside for later) and add the reserved sauce. Wipe roasting pan clean of grease, add Swiss chard, toss in 4 tablespoons oil, salt and pepper.

Place Swiss chard in the center of 6 plates, add your favorite mashed potatoes in one corner and sliced lamb on top of the chard. Spoon sauce over the lamb and add some garlic cloves. Garnish with rosemary sprig and serve immediately.

2 single lamb racks; eye removed, bones chopped

1 medium onion

1 large carrot, peeled and trimmed

1 stalk of celery, washed and trimmed

6 peppercorns

2 bay leaves

3 cups veal or chicken stock

6 cups water

coarse salt

pepper

1 pound Swiss Chard

6 tablespoons olive oil

1 1/2 tablespoons chopped fresh rosemary

12 garlic cloves

mashed potatoes

6 sprigs fresh rosemary

Star Anise

1485 West 12th Ave.
Vancouver, BC
(604) 737-1485

This elegant south Granville eatery has been touted by the US magazine "Gourmet" as one of the best in North America in 1996. Other awards include Best Restaurant in 1994 and 1995 (Vancouver Magazine) and Best Service-Oriented Restaurant 1997 by Tourism Vancouver. Head Chef and co-owner, Julian Bond moved to Canada from London five years ago. Renowned for his imaginative combinations of tastes and textures, Bond changes the dishes on the menu—which can range from Sumptuous Salmon Roasted with Beurre Blanc sauce to an exotic Filet of Ostrich—every few months. By frequently shedding his head-chef clothes and spending a few hours clearing tables, Bond ensures that good cooking and good business go hand in hand. Reservations recommended.

Emu grilled and served with a Mushroom and Potato Torte

Grilled Emu

Making the Potato and Mushroom Pie Filling: In a large saucepan, reduce stock, red wine, 3 tablespoons, roasted garlic, shallots and 1/4 cup chopped parsley. Simmer over medium heat and cook until reduction will coat the back of a spoon (approximately 20 minutes). Add potatoes and mushrooms, salt and pepper to taste. Stir in remaining parsley. Remove two tablespoons of sauce and set aside.

Making the Pie: Lay pastry in a small bowl or mold, add cool filling and top with more pastry. Brush with eggwash and bake at 350 degrees for 15 minutes.

Grilling Steaks: Rub steaks with olive oil and sauce that was set aside. Grill until well-seared on surface, about 5 minutes. Then cook for a further 2 to 3 minutes on each side until steak reaches desired doneness. (This would be medium-rare, depending on thickness.)

Brush steaks with sauce and leave to rest for a few minutes in a warm place. Slice steak across the grain, position on top of the pie on a serving plate. Spoon remaining sauce around, garnish with toasted pistachios, sunflower seeds and watercress. Serve.

2 cups emu stock

2 cups dry red wine, preferably Piñot Noir

1/2 cup garlic cloves, roasted

1/2 cup shallots, chopped

1/2 cup fresh parsley, chopped

1 dash salt, to taste

1 dash fresh ground black pepper, to taste

1/4 cup toasted pistachios, chopped fine

1/4 cup toasted sunflower seeds, chopped fine

1 1/2 pounds emu rump, cut in 5/6 ounce steaks

1 pound potato, diced and blanched

1 pound shiitake mushrooms, sliced and cooked

8 ounces pastry dough

2 tablespoons olive or corn oil

4 sprigs watercress, for garnish

Le Gavroche
Restaurant

Le Gavroche
1616 Alberni St.
Vancouver, BC
(604) 685-3924

Le Gavroche is set in a gently refurbished two-story Victorian house with a fireplace, an upstairs terrace and a sweeping view of Vancouver's Coast Mountains and breathtaking harbour. With a private dining room on the main floor, Le Gavroche can accommodate private parties or business groups with fine European flair. For lovers of food, wine and romance, Le Gavroche is first choice for intimate dining. Avant garde twists to classic French cuisine combined with sensuous simplistic sauces, the lightest natural stocks and uncommon aromatic herbs, provide a dining experience like none other. Among the finest desserts served, "Madame's" Lili Cake is a pâtisserie triumph unequaled anywhere.

Fresh-shelled lobster with Thai curry, lemon grass and coconut milk

Homard au Curry

Steam the lobster until color turns red. Shell the lobster and the claws and reserve them on a warm plate. In a large sauté pan, add the shallots, lemon grass, bay leaves, fennel seeds, lobster stock, peppercorns, Thai curry, heavy cream, cayenne and coconut milk. Reduce the liquid by half over medium-high heat. Strain the liquid through a fine strainer and return to the pan to simmer. Reduce by half again. In a sauté pan, cook the carrot and leek in 1/3 cup of water and 1 teaspoon butter for 3 minutes and then strain. Add lobster to the sauce and simmer for 2 minutes. Serve the lobster in shell with julienne of vegetables.

2 2 pound lobsters

1 teaspoon red Thai curry

1 teaspoon Szechuan peppercorns

1 cup lobster stock

1/2 cup coconut milk

2 bay leaves

1 teaspoon minced shallots

1 lemon grass

1 pinch cayenne

20 fennel seeds

1/2 cup heavy cream

1 leek, julienned

1 medium carrot, julienned

1 teaspoon butter

8

Salmon House on the Hill
2229 Folkestone Way
West Vancouver, BC
(604) 926-3212

the
SALMON HOUSE
aldergrilled fresh seafood

Voted "Best Seafood Restaurant in Vancouver" by critics and locals. Reflecting the best of the Pacific Northwest for over 21 years. The Salmon House is internationally renowned for its sensational ocean view, unique West Coast cooking style, and award-winning wine cellar. Chef Dan, "The Aldermeister," Atkinson's expertise on the alderwood grill, commitment to the Pacific Northwest, and love of cooking is apparent in his menu content and food preparation. From his formal training through local apprenticeships, Dan's primary influence has been from the West Coast. He is truly a "BC product" of whom the Salmon House is very proud! Reservations recommended.

A combination of textures from the crust to the prawns to the wonderful citrus zip.

Garlic and Herb-Crusted Salmon

Sauce: Heat olive oil in a sauté pan. Add onion, peppers, tomato, cayenne, salt and pepper to taste. Simmer 1 minute and add lemon and lime juice. Add stock and reduce by half. Add prawns and simmer 2 minutes.

Combine bread crumbs, salt, pepper, parmesan, garlic, thyme and parsley. Mix evenly and keep refrigerated. Dry off the salmon with a towel, brush with egg and press on garlic breadcrumb mixture. Pour 2 tablespoons olive oil and 1 tablespoon of butter in the sauté pan. When butter starts to brown, add salmon, crustside down. Cook 2 minutes and turn over. Finish in 450 degree oven for 5 minutes. Place sauce on plate, lay salmon over sauce and top with prawns. Sprinkle with chopped chives and serve.

6 cups bread crumbs

1 tablespoon each salt and black pepper

1 tablespoon minced garlic

6 tablespoons grated parmesan cheese

1 tablespoon each, fresh thyme and parsley

1 tablespoon olive oil

3 tablespoons minced red pepper

1 tablespoon tomato concasse

2 tablespoons minced onion

pinch cayenne pepper

1 teaspoon each of lemon and lime juice

3 tiger prawns, butterflied

1/4 cup fish stock

8 ounces fillets of salmon

egg wash

10

The Hermitage
115-1025 Robson Street
Vancouver, BC
(604) 689-3237

Herve Martin, chef/owner of the Hermitage Restaurant, received his training in France. He served as the private chef to King Leopold of Belgium and worked as executive chef at some of the finest hotels in Europe, the United States and Canada. As a Chevaliers du Tastevin, a member of the Chaine des Rôtisseurs and other associations, he brings an unforgettable mix of knowledge and artistry to French dining. Recent awards include "Restaurant of the Year," "Best French" and "Best Wine List" from the 1997 Vancouver Magazine Awards and "America's Top Table Award - Reader's Favourite" from Gourmet Magazine 1997. Lunch is served Monday through Friday and dinner every night. Phone ahead for reservations. There is easy parking beneath the restaurant and we are within easy walking distance of all major downtown hotels and theatres.

Duck Magret with wild mushrooms and armagnac sauce

Duck Magret

Season the breast of Muscovy duck with salt and pepper. Place skin side down in skillet. Sauté on medium heat for 4 to 5 minutes. Flip over and cook skin side up for 2 to 3 minutes. Remove duck from skillet to a warming plate. Drain grease from pan. Sauté shallots for 1 minute, then add the sliced chanterelles and stir for 2 more minutes. Deglaze by adding armagnac. Add white wine and stock. Bring sauce to a boil and add cream. Reduce and remove from burner. Monte with butter, (whisk butter into sauce). Season to taste. Slice duck breast very thinly and fan onto plates. Top with sauce and serve with vegetables of your choice.

1 duck magret (breast of Muscovy duck)

2 ounces armagnac (or cognac)

2 cups fresh chanterelles mushrooms

1 ounce shallots, chopped

1 ounce white wine

4 ounces duck or veal stock

1/2 cup cream

3 ounces butter, room temperature

salt and pepper

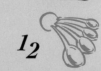

12

La Belle Auberge

La Belle Auberge
4856 - 48th Avenue
Ladner, BC
(604) 946-7717

La Belle Auberge Restaurant has been in operation for the last 18 years and is situated in the small town of Ladner, a short distance from Vancouver. The building has been designated a Heritage House and contains many beautiful antiques and artifacts. The style is that of a French country inn and the service is impeccable. Menus change frequently and feature many local products cooked in the unique style of the restaurant's owner and chef, Bruno Marti. Chef Bruno Marti has achieved many accolades throughout his career. He was a member of the World Champion Team Canada—the grand winners of the Culinary Olympics held in Frankfurt in 1984. Most recently, he was Team manager for Canada's National Culinary Olympic Team that competed in the 1996 World Culinary Olympics in Berlin, winning three gold medals. In June, he was voted the "Canadian National Chef of the Year" by his peers at the Annual Meeting of the Canadian Federation of Chefs and Cooks.

...with lettuce, tomato, basil, reduced balsamic vinegar and goat cheese

Vegetable Terrine

Sauté aubergine in garlic and oil. Place in oven for 20 minutes. Purée, adding a little water if needed. Sauté shallots in oil for 1 minute. Add beans and 1/4 cup water. Season to taste; simmer until cooked but still crisp. Cool. In a few drops of oil and water, simmer squash in oven at 400 degrees until tender, about 10 minutes. Turn once, season with herbs. Repeat with celery root, cover; cook in oven for 30 minutes. Sauté mushrooms in a little oil and water. Season with salt, pepper and garlic. Blanch leek (10 minutes) and carrot (3 minutes) in boiling salted water. Cool in ice water. Melt packet of gelatin according to instructions. Line mold with plastic wrap. Add carrot slices, placing across mold with excess hanging over edges. Brush with gelatin. Layer squash over carrots and brush with gelatin. Layer tomatoes, celery, aubergine, beans (lengthwise), leeks, mushrooms, etc. Alternate ingredients to give color combination. Brush each layer with gelatin. After brushing final layer, fold carrots over into gelatin to seal. Fold in plastic wrap. Place weight on top; refrigerate at least one day.

4 large carrots, peeled, cut into long thin strips the length of the carrot

200 grams aubergine, cubed

100 grams green beans

200 grams butternut squash, peeled, deseeded, slice lengthwise 1 centimeter thick

200 grams tomatoes, peeled, deseeded, halved

200 grams celery root (European), peeled, slice lenghwise 1 centimenter thick

100 grams shiitake mushrooms, whole, stems removed

1 clove garlic, chopped

fresh herbs, chopped (oregano, thyme, basil)

2 medium leeks, cleaned, left whole

chopped shallots

olive oil

gelatin

Terrine mold - 10 by 10 by 30 centimeters with lid, preferably earthenware

14

Allegro Café
888 Nelson Street
Vancouver, BC
(604) 683-8485

If a restaurant can be called a flirt, this is it! Allegro Café is the secret of Vancouver. Tucked away in the courtyard of an office tower across from the Law Courts, this restaurant will warm you with its intimate appeal. Inside you'll find the highest level of personal service, savoury dishes and wines that complement your dining experience. Allegro Café has been highlighted in city newspapers and rates highly as a city favourite, while maintaining reasonable prices. Owner Michael Mitton is devoted to providing your dining pleasure, while Chef Barbara Reese shows her passion for cooking, in everything from your opening bread basket to your satisfying dessert, something you must save room for! Each meal starts with a basket of bread loaded with Barbara's twisted cheese straws, flaky scones, foccacia and sweet poppy seed cake, to name a few. Next open your senses with Barbara's never rivaled soups, such as the Tomato Basil or Smoked Salmon Bisque. Entrée menus are complemented by daily tantalizing "specials!" We could go on and on, but we must resist. Try everything! One can only return again and again to be fully satisfied.

A blend of fruit and juices enhance the flavour of this charbroiled breast of chicken.

Pollo con Frutti

Charbroil chicken breasts until surface is well seared and juices run clear. In a pot, heat orange juice, lemon juice, orange liqueur, brown sugar, and orange slices for approximately 4 to 5 minutes. Add remaining fruit slices and pine nuts. Lay chicken breasts on plates and spoon sauce over them.

Serves 2.

2 8 ounce boneless breasts of chicken

4 ounces freshly squeezed orange juice

2 tablespoons lemon juice

4 teaspoons orange liqueur

3 ounces brown sugar

2 ounces mango

2 ounces oranges, peeled and sliced

2 ounces pine nuts

2 large ripe kiwi

2 ounces raspberries or blueberries

4 large strawberries

900 West
900 West Georgia Street
Vancouver, BC
(604) 684-3131

900 West Restaurant and Wine Bar is recognized throughout the culinary world for its innovative cuisine, dynamic wine program and trend-setting style in restaurant dining. The menu highlights the best of British Columbia's culinary bounty with the creation of "new classic cuisine," emphasizing simplicity and purity in preparation, condiments, and most importantly—flavour. To complement the menu is a comprehensive and dynamic wine program that will appeal to the curious and connoisseur alike. A testimonial to the achievements of 900 West are the endless prestigious awards including: Wine Spectator's 1997 "Award of Excellence;" the Vancouver Playhouse 1996 International Wine Festival "Best Wine By the Glass Selection;" and one of the 1997 Vancouver Magazine Restaurant's "Best New Restaurants" Awards. Be it a casual gathering, a business meeting or the celebration of a special occasion, 900 West is the perfect choice for locals and visitors.

seared veal chop served with a fig and pear risotto.

Grilled Peppered Veal Chop

To make risotto, bring water, sugar and lemon juice to a boil. Add pear and bring back to a boil. Add figs and remove from heat. In a separate pan, add butter, shallots and lightly sweat off without color. Add pearl barley and a little chicken stock. Boil until all liquid has evaporated, then add a little more chicken stock. Continue this process until all the stock is gone or until barley is cooked to taste. Add fig and pear mixture and reduce until all liquid has evaporated. Season to taste. To make sauce, sweat off shallots and green peppercorn without any oil, then add white wine and reduce. When reduced, add chicken stock and repeat. Add veal stock, season and reduce to required consistency. Sear veal chops on hot grill or pan to provide color. Place chops in hot oven for 6 to 8 minutes or until cooked to preferred doneness. Julienne leeks, place in a pan of hot olive oil and fry until crisp. Place risotto in 3 to 4 inch ring at top of plates and rest veal chop bone off risotto. Garnish sauce with tomato and chive garnish. Pour sauce around and place leeks over the top of the risotto.

2 10 ounce veal chops

1 medium leek

Risotto

2 fresh figs

1/2 pear

1/2 ounce sugar

1 cup water

1 shallot, chopped

2 ounces pearl barley

1/4 ounce butter

2 cups chicken stock, hot

1 lemon, juiced

Sauce

1 shallot, chopped

1 cup white wine

1 teaspoon green peppercorns

1/2 tomato, diced

1 teaspoon chopped chives

1 1/2 cups veal stock

18

The Cannery Seafood Restaurant
2205 Commissioner Street
Vancouver, BC
(604) 254-9606

Entering its 26th year, The Cannery Seafood restaurant is one of Vancouver's dining landmarks. Located on the waterfront and specializing in fresh seafood, The Cannery's picturesque setting overlooking the harbour and North Shore mountains assures guests of a memorable evening. The Cannery's commitment to excellence has garnered praise from both its guests as well as the media. Winning Vancouver Magazines Reader's poll of "Best Seafood Restaurant," Where Magazine's "Most Memorable Meal Award," and the prestigious "Best Award of Excellence" from Wine Spectator Magazine confirms The Cannery is Vancouver's premiere seafood restaurant. At the heart of The Cannery's commitment to excellence is Executive Chef Frederic Couton. Trained in French and Continental techniques, Frederic returns to Vancouver after a successful turn at world-renowned international hotels. Combining the Pacific Northwest's outstanding fresh ingredients with his global influences, Frederic's creativity has raised The Cannery's menu to a new level.

Seared Giant Scallops

Halve fennel, remove the hard centre, cut remaining into small cubes. Clean basil, remove stem, blanch leaves in boiling water for 5 seconds. Cool down in cold water. In blender mix basil with 4 ounces of oil for 1 minute until oil turns green. Strain, reserve only the oil. Preheat deep fryer to 350 degrees. Peel taro and carrots. With a mandolin, slice into a ribbon 1/2 inch wide and 6 inches long. Place in fryer for about 1 minute until golden colour. Place on paper towel; add touch of salt. Reserve. In a medium-hot saucepan add 1/4 ounce oil, fennel cubes, sauté for 2 minutes. Add 1/2 cup water, cover, cook for 5 minutes. Finish with 1/2 tablespoon butter. Salt and pepper to taste. Preheat oven to 390 degrees. Halve tomatoes, remove seeds, dice. Reserve. Season scallops with salt and pepper. Sauté in pan on medium heat with one teaspoon of oil until golden colour. Place in oven for 2 minutes (depending on scallop size). Reserve. In a pan over medium heat mix the fennel and tomato cubes with 1 tablespoon butter. Place in middle of plate with scallops on top.

In a small bowl, mix caviar and reserved seasoned oil very gently. Add mixture around scallops, add taro and carrot ribbons, garnish with chervil.

1 1/2 pounds clean giant scallops

3 pounds fennel

2 tomatoes

1 taro

1 carrot

5 ounces extra virgin olive oil

1/2 ounce basil

2 ounces butter

4 pieces chervil

1/2 ounce caviar (salmon and beluga)

20

Horizons
100 Centennial Way
Burnaby, BC
(604) 299-1155

HORIZONS restaurant
"Aldergilled Fresh Seafood & Steaks"

A Burnaby tradition for over 11 years, Horizons offers a dining experience not easily matched elsewhere. Nestled in the natural beauty of Burnaby Mountain Park, Horizons boasts the most spectacular, panoramic view in the city. Coupled with a comfortable ambiance, award winning wine list and an exciting menu featuring seafood and steaks from the alderwood grill, Horizons is a favourite of locals and tourists alike. Diverse, extensive experience and a passion for creative cuisine makes John Garrett one of Vancouver's most exciting chefs. John applies his sixteen years of accumulated skills to produce dishes that are a delight to both the taste and sight. His commitment to fresh, top quality ingredients and his flair with the alderwood grill is reflected on his seasonally changing menus.

Pan-roasted breast of chicken with pasilla chili cornmeal crust.

Breast of Chicken

In a stainless steel bowl mix together marinade ingredients. Place breasts in marinade, cover and refrigerate at least 6 hours. Mix together cornmeal crust ingredients and set aside. Preheat oven to 375 degrees. Remove chicken breasts from marinade and let drain for a couple of minutes. Heat 2 to 3 tablespoons olive oil in a large cast iron skillet until it is quite hot, but not to the smoking point. Lightly dredge chicken in the cornmeal crust (both sides) and place in the hot pan. Sear for about 4 to 5 minutes each side, then place the pan in the oven for 8 to 10 minutes until chicken is just firm to the touch and the juices are clear. Serve immediately with your favourite fresh tomato or fruit salsa.

4 6 ounce boneless skinless chicken breasts

Marinade

2 cups extra virgin olive oil

1/4 cup balsamic vinegar

1 clove garlic, chopped

2 tablespoons fresh herbs, chopped (thyme, oregano and basil)

Cornmeal Crust

1 cup cornmeal

1/4 cup all-purpose flour

2 tablespoons pasilla chili powder

1 tablespoon cumin seeds, toasted and ground

sea salt to taste

freshly ground black pepper to taste

Moustache Café 5th Avenue
2118 Burrard Street
Vancouver, BC
(604) 739-1990

In the heart of Kitsilano, there is a Mediterranean oasis, a place where the cuisine of the Middle East and Southern Europe have met and married the fresh ingredients that abound locally to form a tantalizing blend of the Old and New Worlds. Finish off the evening with a glass from the wide range of ports or from the selection of 28 single malt scotches. The wine list is superb, with a reserve list for more experimentation. The Moustache Café takes the best of the Old World and combines it with the best of the New World for a dining experience you will never forget.

Roasted lamb sirloin with nicoise olives and herbs served on golden potato cake.

Lamb Sirloin Nicoise

Cut lamb into 4 pieces. Cover with olive oil, herbs, bay leaves and peppercorns. Marinate overnight. Preheat oven to 450 degrees. Peel and grate potatoes. Heat 1 tablespoon olive oil to medium high in frying pan. Place a thin layer of grated potato into pan and fry until golden. Flip and brown other side, drain on kitchen towel. Preheat 2 cups of vegetable oil in deep frying pan. Place eggplant into hot oil and deep fry until crisp. Drain on kitchen towel; sprinkle with icing sugar. Toss zucchini and tomato in olive oil and salt and pepper. Grill on each side, season. Drain lamb, season with salt and pepper. Heat frying pan to medium high and brown each side of lamb. Place lamb into oven for 7 minutes, then remove and let rest for 5 minutes. Place the green beans, layered zucchini and tomato onto four hot plates. Then place potato cake into centre of plate as shown. Slice lamb and place on top of potato cake. Garnish with 1 tablespoon of baba ghanoush and two Japanese eggplant chips on each. Further garnish with pan juices from lamb and some extra virgin olive oil.

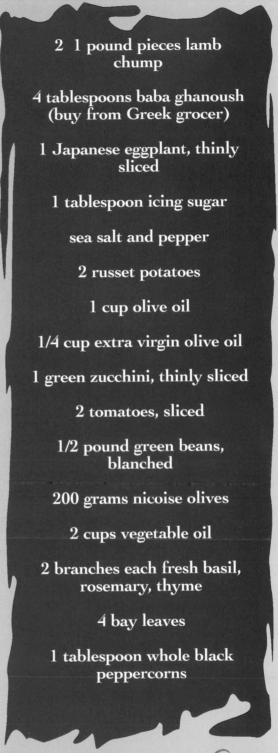

2 1 pound pieces lamb chump

4 tablespoons baba ghanoush (buy from Greek grocer)

1 Japanese eggplant, thinly sliced

1 tablespoon icing sugar

sea salt and pepper

2 russet potatoes

1 cup olive oil

1/4 cup extra virgin olive oil

1 green zucchini, thinly sliced

2 tomatoes, sliced

1/2 pound green beans, blanched

200 grams nicoise olives

2 cups vegetable oil

2 branches each fresh basil, rosemary, thyme

4 bay leaves

1 tablespoon whole black peppercorns

Mangiamo
1116 Mainland Street
Vancouver, BC
(604) 687-1116

Mangiamo! The food keeps people coming back to this chic eatery in trendy Yaletown. A delightful design by Chef Ken Bogas, formerly of Saltimbocca, creates an environment and menu which is both vibrant and elegant. Parchment-colored walls, dark woods with soft light emanating from the Tucsan garden patio, and perfectly white linen table cloths complement this unique design. Food favorites include his many preparations of Ahi Tuna, and Grilled Filet of Angus Beef with tempura onion rings and gorgonzola mashed potatoes. Ken's other passion is wine and his list features over 400 selections, which he delights in pairing with any and all of the ever-changing menu items. Ciao, Mangiamo!

Ahi Tuna Sashimi

To prepare dressing, combine mayonnaise, honey, Dijon mustard and wasabi in a mixing bowl and blend with a wire whisk. Add remaining dressing ingredients and mix again. Place dressing in plastic squeeze bottle with small tip.

To prepare the tuna, season tuna steaks with salt and pepper and then brush with vegetable oil. Dredge all sides in sesame seeds. Heat pan over medium-high heat with a small amount of vegetable oil. Add tuna steaks one at a time. Lightly brown both sides for about 20 seconds on each side. Place on paper towel to absorb excess oil. Squeeze dressing in a lovely design on dinner plates. Thinly slice tuna steaks and gently place on displayed sauce. Garnish with tobiko, if desired. (Recommended) This dish is best when accompanied by garlic mashed potatoes and steamed seasonal vegetables. Serve with dry or off-dry Gewürztraminer or New World Pinot Noir.

4 6 ounce ahi tuna filets

1/4 cup toasted white sesame seeds

1/4 cup black sesame seeds

1 tablespoon vegetable oil

salt and pepper to taste

Tobiko (flying fish roe)

Dressing

1/2 cup real mayonnaise

1 tablespoon honey

1 tablespoon Dijon mustard

1 tablespoon prepared wasabi

juice of 1 fresh lime

6 drops sesame oil

Raintree at the Landing
375 Water Street
Vancouver, BC
(604)688-5570

The Raintree at the Landing is Vancouver's award winning Pacific Northwest Restaurant. Thousands of locals and visitors flock to the Raintree every year because of its premier reputation for quality food, an extensive Pacific Northwest wine list and unparalleled service. Executive Chef Bradley Cleases' menu focuses on everything that British Columbia has to offer. Fresh seafood is in abundance. A bounty of quality meats, fresh vegetables, fruits and berries allow for a menu that will please a simple palate or the most adventurous diner. The Raintree is proud of its relationship with many of the local farmers in the Lower Mainland. It is through these lasting relationships that they have been able to ensure the quality standards that the menu consistently offers. Visit the restaurant and enjoy the breathtaking view of the Vancouver's Trade and Convention Centre, its beautiful harbour and the mountains in the distance. Relax and enjoy the rustic elegance of the dining room in one of Vancouver's most prized heritage buildings.

Porcini Dusted Lamb Rack

To make mushroom demi, roughly chop carrots, onions and celery and sauté until browned with a bay leaf. Add vegetables to beef stock and bring to a boil. Reduce by half. In separate pan sauté shallots and fresh mushrooms and set aside. Strain stock through sieve to remove vegetables. Add cooked mushrooms and simmer on low heat. Grind dried mushrooms in a domestic coffee grinder until the consistency of fine powder. Mix mushroom powder, pepper and salt to make mushroom dust. Coat each rack with mushroom dust and sear in skillet over high heat. Finish rack in a 400 degree oven for 15 minutes or until preferred doneness. Remove from oven and cut into chops. Serve with mushroom demi.

4 10 ounce small lamb racks (cleaned and frenched by a butcher)

10 ounces dried porcini mushrooms

1 teaspoon salt

1 teaspoon black pepper

1/2 cup chantrelle mushrooms

1/2 cup oyster mushrooms

1 medium sized onion

2 medium carrots

2 stalks celery

1 bay leaf

2 shallots, finely diced

4 to 5 quarts beef stock

A Kettle of Fish
900 Pacific St.
Vancouver, BC
(604) 682-6661
www.andersonrestaurants.com/kettle.html

Famed for its "always fresh fish" and the pleasure of greenery-filled comfort, A Kettle of Fish has been a Vancouver legend since 1979. Numerous seafood selections are offered, changing daily. Choose a West Coast catch, or something delectable from the oceans of the world. Each dish is carefully prepared to enhance the flavour that only freshness can bring. From the land, Executive Chef Matthew Keen also offers steak, chicken and veal with pastas and salads. The featured recipe, West Coast Bouillabaisse, is our own version, simmered with flamed lemon pepper crab, fresh shellfish, seafood, julienne of vegetables and flavoured with Pernod. A fine bottle of Zinfandel would accompany this dish beautifully, offering the perfect marriage of flavours. Or make your own selection from our excellent list of wines assembled by General Manager Michael Popove. Come and see why the readers of "Where" magazine have voted A Kettle of Fish one of "Vancouver's Top 10 Restaurants," two years running. Reservations are recommended.

seafood and vegetables simmered in a delectable fish broth.

West Coast Bouillabaisse

To make fish broth, rinse fish bones well. In a large pot add water, fish bones, 2 rough cut carrots, 1 rough cut onion, 2 rough cut celery stalks, garlic and bay leaves. Simmer for 1/2 hour, strain into a large heavy bottomed pot (large enough to accommodate the shellfish) and let cool.

Add tomato paste, tomato, herbs, hot sauce, Worcestershire, wine, salt and pepper. Simmer for 1/2 hour and re-season if necessary.

Rinse the clams. Rinse and de-beard the mussels. Cut the assorted fish into 1/2 inch pieces. Cook, clean and chill the crab. Julienne the remaining vegetables (cut into match stick sized pieces).

Add in the following order: clams, mussels, fish, crab and vegetables. Bring to a rapid boil and then simmer for 10 to 12 minutes, or until mussels are open. Sprinkle each bowl with chopped parsley and enjoy!

3 pounds fresh or frozen fish bones
6 cups cold water
3 medium carrots
2 large onions
3 celery stalks
6 garlic cloves, rough cut
3 bay leaves
1/4 cup tomato paste
1 large tomato, diced
3/4 teaspoon each thyme, basil, oregano
2 tablepoons Worcestershire sauce
1 tablepoon Louisiana hot sauce
1/2 cup dry white wine
salt and pepper to taste
1 pound whole mussels
1 pound whole clams
1 pound assorted boneless fish pieces
2 whole dungeness crabs
1/2 head fennel*
1 cup leeks
1/4 bunch parsley, chopped fine

Pernod may be substituted for fennel if unavailable or if a stronger flavour is desired.

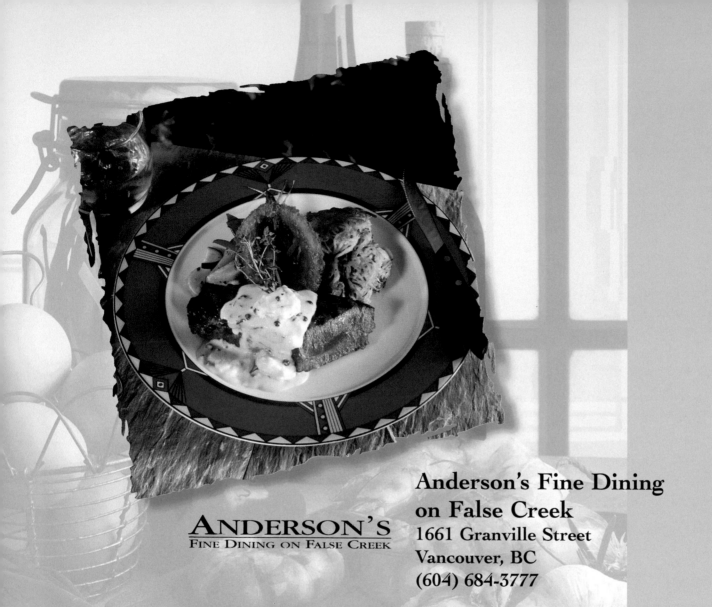

Anderson's Fine Dining on False Creek

ANDERSON'S
FINE DINING ON FALSE CREEK

Anderson's Fine Dining on False Creek
1661 Granville Street
Vancouver, BC
(604) 684-3777

Anderson's brings the understated elegance of a private club dining room to one of Vancouver's finest restaurants. The décor is warm and tasteful, the ever-changing view of False Creek an added delight.

Beef is the featured entrée. Renowned for their Prime Rib of well-aged Alberta beef, Anderson's steaks are becoming a legend of their own. From the Filet Mignon and Rib Eye to a 20-ounce Porterhouse, each is cut from the finest beef available in North America, grilled to exact customer taste and presented with flair. At Anderson's, the beef lover's quest for the perfect steak is finally over! Other choices include fresh seafood and continental dishes creatively prepared.

Anderson's welcomes group functions and is a favorite for wedding receptions. 170 can be seated, or 300 hosted for cocktails and hors d'oeuvres. Open for lunch and dinner. Ample free parking. Reservations recommended.

The hottest sizzle in town these days is that of great steaks

The New York Stilton

In a bowl, cream together the cheese and butter until the mixture is smooth. In a saucepan, boil the wine with the peppercorns until it is reduced by about 1 tablespoon. Add the cream and heat the liquid until it is reduced by 1/2. Reduce the heat to moderately low, whisk the cheese mixture a little at a time into the cream mixture, then whisk in the parsley. Remove from heat and keep the sauce warm.

Preheat your grill to very hot. Pat steaks dry and season with salt and pepper. Reduce heat to medium-low and grill steaks for 4 to 5 minutes on each side for medium-rare. Top with Stilton sauce.

Accompanied here with horseradish potato cakes, fresh vegetables and a sourdough onion ring.

1/2 pound Stilton cheese, softened

1/2 cup unsalted butter, softened

1 1/2 cups dry white wine

4 teaspoons freeze-dried green peppercorns

1 cup heavy cream

4 teaspoons fresh parsley leaves, minced

4 8 to 10 ounce cuts of the finest AAA North American beef available

The Fleuri Restaurant at The Sutton Place Hotel

845 Burrard Street
Vancouver, BC
(604) 682-5511

Step inside the highly acclaimed Fleuri Restaurant at the AAA Five Diamond-rated Sutton Place Hotel and let Executive Chef Kai Lerman dazzle and delight even the most discerning palate. His passion for dining is evident in the artful presentations, flavours and textures of his classical, Continental cooking style. Lobster and Scallop Chartreuse, one of his signature dishes, is a favourite starter among Chef Kai's epicurean followers. Diners at the Fleuri savor Chef Kai's menus, featuring the bounty of the Pacific Northwest, amidst the grandeur of a European manor complete with floor-length floral-printed tablecloths, damask wall coverings and original artwork. Located on the lobby level, the Fleuri Restaurant is open from 6 a.m. to 11 p.m. daily. Reservations are highly recommended. Live nightly piano entertainment. Valet parking.

A culinary dance of lobster, scallops, Granny Smith apples and English Cucumber.

Lobster and Scallop Chartreuse

Combine the mayonnaise, ketchup, stock, tabasco, salt, pepper, coriander and chives in a small bowl. Arrange cucumber slices around the inside of the ring in a layered pattern. Cook the lobsters in boiling salted water for approximately 8 minutes. Shell the lobster meat and diagonally slice the tail. Dice the claw, knuckle and the top and end of the tail into 1/4 inch pieces. Sauté the scallops lightly in olive oil. Cool and combine with diced lobster and apples. Add half of the mayonnaise mixture to the seafood and mix to combine. Place a toast round in each of the rings and top with the diced seafood mixture. Arrange the sliced lobster pieces in a spiral design on top. Drizzle with some extra virgin olive oil and fresh lemon juice. Carefully remove each plastic ring. Garnish the lobster chartreuse with some fresh salad greens and finish with the remainder of the sauce. Serves 4 persons as an appetizer course.

4 plastic rings, 3 inches in diameter and 1 inch high

2 pounds lobster

1 pound Calico scallops

2 Granny Smith apples, peeled and chopped in 1/4 inch dice

4 slices white bread, toasted and cut in 3 inch rounds

1 English cucumber, finely sliced

1/2 cup mayonnaise

2 tablespoons ketchup

1/4 cup chilled lobster stock

dash of Tabasco

salt and pepper to taste

1/4 teaspoon coriander

1 teaspoon chives, chopped

fresh lemon juice

34

Aqua Riva
200 Granville Street
Vancouver, BC
(604) 683-5599

AQUA AR RIVA
Wood-fired Rôtisserie
& Seafood Grill

The newest arrival on Vancouver's culinary waterfront is a sleek and inventive addition that artfully mirrors the city's growing love affair with the cruise ship. With sweeping harbor scenery, curvaceous, sexy decor, state-of-the-art kitchen with de rigeur wood-burning ovens and rotisserie, this is the place. Besides being one of the city's most imaginative chefs, Deb Connors is also one of the most down-to-earth. This inventive executive chef at Aqua Riva has quietly positioned herself among the ranks of Vancouver's most notable chefs. Her diverse background and mastery of cooking over open flame are apparent in the fabulous meats and seafood emerging from her wood-burning oven, grill and rotisserie. Deb's commitment to fresh, seasonal products from the West Coast, combined with her natural culinary skills, make her one of Vancouver's most exciting and talented chefs.

Fraser Valley Lamb Salad with a
Savory Vinaigrette and New Potatoes.

Lamb Loin in Vinaigrette

Marinate lamb for at least 4 hours—preferably overnight—in refrigerator. Sweat onion and garlic in 2 tablespoons olive oil until soft and translucent. Add tomato purée and deglaze with vinegar. Reduce by 2/3 over low heat. Add red wine, reduce by 1/2, strain and reduce to 3 tablespoons. Whisk in 1/2 cup olive oil. Season with salt and pepper.

Cut potatoes in rounds at least 1/2 inch thick, skin on. Lightly blanch, then sear in olive oil until colored. Season with salt and pepper, set aside and keep warm.

Heat 3 tablespoons olive oil in pan over high heat. Sear lamb loin to medium-rare, about 3 minutes per side, set aside and keep warm. Lightly fry pancetta bacon. Cook shallots in olive oil until crisp. Slice lamb thinly, place in semi-circle on plate, alternating with potato slices. Place wild greens in center. Drizzle with vinaigrette, garnish with pancetta and shallots.

2 8 ounce lamb loins, trimmed

8 small red potatoes

4 large shallots, chopped

2 ounces pancetta bacon, julienned

4 ounces wild greens

Marinade

1/2 cup red wine

4 tablespoons balsamic vinegar

1 teaspoon cracked pepper

2 cloves garlic, thinly sliced

1 bay leaf

1 teaspoon each fresh thyme, oregano and parsley

1/4 cup olive oil

Red Wine Vinaigrette

1 small onion, peeled and chopped

12 cloves garlic, peeled and chopped

1/2 cup canned, puréed tomato

4 tablespoons balsamic vinegar

2 cups red wine

salt and pepper

The Boathouse Restaurants
1795 Beach Avenue
Vancouver, BC
(604) 669-2225

Pick a favourite waterfront location in and around the Lower Mainland of British Columbia and there's every chance that right in the middle of it you'll find a Boathouse Restaurant... in always spectacular English Bay, across from the beach in White Rock, on the Fraser River in New Westminster and Richmond, or close to where the ferries dock at Horseshoe Bay. The Boathouse has claimed neighbourhood and regional fame as the home of fresh West Coast Salmon and other great local seafood, all served with a waterfront view by people who make you feel welcome. Seafood at its best! A change of taste? Nothing better than Boathouse spit-roasted prime rib! Settle in any day or night of the week with great wines or a frosted glass of Boathouse exclusive Killer Whale Ale, all in casual surroundings, all in a friendly place.

Peppered scallops with sweet soy sauce and Wasabi potatoes

Black Pepper Sea Scallops

Place scallops in strainer, drain excess liquid. Place scallops in a bowl, sprinkle generously with black pepper until coated. Lightly coat scallops with flour, shake off excess.

In a large skillet, heat oil until very hot. Reduce heat, add scallops, sauté quickly, turning over once, cook approximately 3 minutes. Add soy sauce and bring to boil, remove from heat.

Mix wasabi powder with 1/4 cup of warm water, dissolve powder. Add wasabi mix to mashed potatoes, a little at a time to taste (you may not want all, it can be quite hot), set aside and keep hot.

Steam green beans and pepper strips; toss with sesame oil, salt and pepper to taste.

Place large scoop of mashed potatoes in the center of a large plate. Place 5 to 6 green beans sticking out of mashed potatoes, and 2 pepper strips criss-crossed over top.

Divide scallops equally and place around each plate. Drizzle a little sauce over scallops.

Sprinkle each plate with toasted sesame seeds. Serve.

Serves 4.

Black Pepper Sea Scallops

1 1/2 pounds large sea scallops

2 tablespoons freshly ground pepper

1/2 cup flour

1/4 cup vegetable oil

3/4 cup sweet soy sauce*

4 servings mashed potatoes**
adding a little garlic and salt while cooking

5 teaspoons wasabi powder*

2 cups whole green beans

8 strips red pepper

1 tablespoon sesame oil

2 tablespoons toasted sesame seeds

*available at Asian food markets
**use a standard mashed potato recipe

38

ARRIVA
ristorante italiano

Arriva Ristorante
1537 Commercial Drive
Vancouver, BC
(604) 251-1177

Vancouver is one of the most culturally diverse cities in North America. It has been described as a city of "neighborhoods." Commercial Drive is considered by many to be one of the most animated neighborhoods. Old World charm meets progressive new trends in art, clothing and most importantly, cuisine. It is here we find "Arriva." High ceilings, tile floors and arched doorways create an atmosphere of a contemporary Mediterranean villa. Enjoy superbly prepared Italian food complemented by a home-cooked touch. Paolo Frau, owner, takes a personal interest in your traditional dining experience.

Breast of turkey with mushrooms in a tomato cream sauce

Tacchino alla Cardinale

To make tomato sauce, crush tomatoes in a mixing bowl. In a shallow wide pan, over high heat, sauté onion in oil until well cooked. Add crushed tomatoes, garlic, basil, bay leaves, chili peppers, oregano, salt and pepper and simmer uncovered on medium heat for 20 minutes, stirring occasionally. Slice turkey breast to 1/4 inch thickness and pound with a mallet until tender. Season to taste with salt and pepper. Roll in flour and shake off excess. In a medium-hot skillet, melt butter. Quickly add turkey and sauté for 2 minutes on each side. Add mushrooms and sauté for another 2 to 3 minutes, flipping turkey occasionally. Add white wine and stir for 1 minute. Add in 1/2 cup tomato sauce and cream. Stir, reduce for 1 minute. Season with white pepper and oregano. Serve immediately with your choice of steamed vegetables.

16 ounces turkey breast

salt

flour

butter

1/2 cup mushrooms, thinly sliced

2 ounces dry white wine

1 ounce heavy cream, 36 percent

Tomato Sauce

400 grams San Marzano Italian tomatoes

2 tablespoons pure olive oil

1/4 cup onion, finely chopped

2 cloves garlic

6 basil leaves, sliced

2 bay leaves

pinch dry red chili peppers

pinch oregano

salt and pepper to taste

C Restaurant
2-1600 Howe Street
Vancouver, BC
(604) 681-1164

Taking seafood to a new level of excellence, Vancouver's finest fish restaurant is located on a wonderful waterfront location across False Creek from Granville Island Market. Owner Harry Kambolis wants everything in the restaurant to be touched by seafood, creating some very interesting combinations. C Restaurant is an exciting new concept in cuisine, menu, presentation and ambiance. Above all, C means exotic food stylings to open your tastes to a contemporary, progressive seafood cuisine. Chef Soren Fakstorp has taken the very best ingredients from around the world and brought them to their full potential. C also features local and imported wines listed by taste categories. C Restaurant is a ground breaking concept that takes seafood dining in Vancouver into a new era.

Saskatoon berry tea-cured salmon gravlax

Salmon Gravlax

Mix salt, sugar and pepper. Spread a quarter of salt mixture evenly on bottom of non-reactive platter or roasting pan. Place one salmon filet, skin side down on the salt mixture. Cover meat side of fish with another quarter of salt mixture and sprinkle evenly with half the berry tea. Cover meat side of other fillet evenly with 1/4 of salt mixture and remaining tea and place meat side down on top of the first filet. Cover whole fish with remaining salt mixture. Invert another platter or pan onto fish to cover. Place something heavy on top of platter to apply pressure and place in refrigerator to marinate for 8 hours. Turn whole fish over and marinate for further 6 hours. Remove salmon from pan. Strain off one cup of the juices. Scrape excess marinade from salmon. To serve, slice the gravlax thinly and serve with dill dressing.

Dressing: Combine all dressing ingredients and mix well. Adjust seasoning with sugar and lemon juice.

1 salmon (approximately 3 1/2 pounds), scaled and filleted, skin on

100 grams pickling (coarse) salt

90 grams white sugar

10 cracked white peppercorns

30 grams Saskatoon berry tea

<u>Berry Dill Dressing</u>

1 cup salmon marinade

1/2 cup sour cream

2 bunches fresh dill, finely chopped

sugar and lemon juice to taste

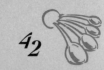

The Bedford House

The Bedford House Restaurant
9272 Glover Road
Fort Langley, BC
(604) 888-2333

The Bedford House provides the perfect end to a casual day of sight seeing in and around historic Fort Langley. Built in 1904, the house remained a private residence until 1975 when the structure was remodeled and converted into a restaurant. Chef-Owner Herb Feischl offers award-winning entrées including salmon, duckling and lamb. Situated on the banks of the Fraser River in a sumptuous flower garden, the stately grounds and grand character of the house are constant reminders of the area's history. The Bedford House invites you to be their guest and share in the special atmosphere that makes your dining experience a truly enjoyable one.

Taste of the Wild

Wild duck breast and venison with juniper berries

Duck and Deer: Rub duck breasts with salt and pepper, 6 juniper berries; marinate in 2 tablespoons oil for at least 3 hours in refrigerator. Cut deer in 3 chop pieces, rub with salt, pepper, thyme, mustard and 6 crushed juniper berries. Marinate in oil for 3 hours in refrigerator.

Heat cast iron pan to smoking, add breasts skin side down until golden. Turn for 2 minutes and finish in 400 degree oven for 10 to 15 minutes. Remove from oven when medium rare. Pan fry deer in hot casserole until evenly browned; finish in hot oven with duck until medium. Allow 10 minutes for meats to rest prior to service. Heat both pans on stove, sprinkle in one tablespoon flour and fill with prepared sauce. Reduce, strain and finish with fresh cream.

Sauce: Heat small casserole and sauté with oil, small chunks of bacon, onions, carrots, parsnip, celery and all trimmings from deer and duck. When browned, add 3 cups stock, two tablespoons cranberry sauce, bay leaf, tomato paste and splash of red wine. Allow mixture to simmer at least one hour; strain.

To Serve: Place sliced duck and parted deer on heated individual plates. Gently pour sauce around meat.

2 Muscovy duck breasts, approximately 800 grams

2 fallow deer racks, approximately 1200 grams

1 cup oil

salt and pepper

dijon mustard

thyme

1 bay leaf

1 teaspoon tomato paste

12 crushed juniper berries

1 carrot

1 stalk celery

1 parsnip

1 small onion

50 grams double smoked bacon

3 cups prepared stock (beef, venison or duck)

2 tablespoons cranberry sauce

1 tablespoon flour

1/2 cup heavy cream

red wine, to taste

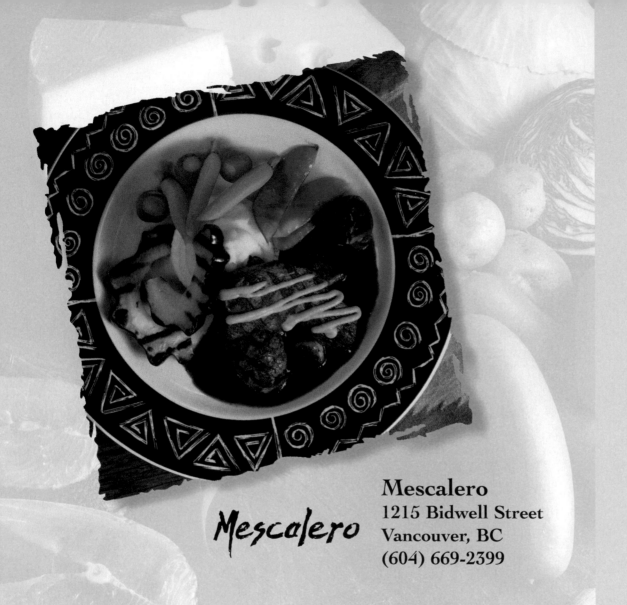

Mescalero

Mescalero
1215 Bidwell Street
Vancouver, BC
(604) 669-2399

Mescalero is located in Vancouver's West End, just one block from the beaches of English Bay. Built into a 1929 California mission-style building that is rich with local history, the restaurant surrounds an open kitchen, using a wood-burning stove as its centrepiece. The rustic decor and innovative cuisine make Mescalero's a hot spot for local and visiting diners. Once rumored to be a brothel in the 1930s, large parties are always welcome to take advantage of the private dining area affectionately known as the Bordello Room, which is appointed with highback leather chairs, a comfortable sofa and a cozy fireplace. Chef James Klassen has created a menu full of cutting-edge recipes and customers find themselves returning for their favourite dishes, but are unable to resist the new additions to the menu. Spicy modern Latin jazz, fresh fruit margaritas and classic martinis are lounge specialties. The distressed walls reveal lives past lived, the candlelit room full of exciting sights, smells and sounds combined to provide a memorable evening at Mescalero. Don't forget to ask your server about the guest who never leaves.

Chile and fresh herb marinated venison with a sun-dried apricot mustard.

Marinated Venison

Place dry marinade ingredients in blender and purée while adding red wine. Slowly add oil to make an emulsion. Place meat in large flat dish with high sides and coat with marinade. Cover and refrigerate 4 to 6 hours. Remove venison from marinade, pat dry. Place on preheated BBQ (spraying grill with non-stick spray). Cook to desired doneness while brushing with remaining marinade. To prepare sauce, sauté whole garlic cloves with a little oil. Add sugar and vegetable stock, then cover and reduce by 2/3. Add beef stock and fresh thyme, reduce by 1/3. To prepare apricot mustard, simmer apricots in water with shallots, garlic and cayenne for 8 to 10 minutes. Drain and reserve liquid. Transfer ingredients to blender, add Dijon mustard and purée until smooth, adding reserved liquid slowly until a mustard-like consistency is reached, then refrigerate. Spoon sauce onto a plate and add meat. Serve with apricot mustard, fresh vegetables and enjoy.

3 pounds fresh venison

Apricot Mustard
1/2 cup sun-dried apricots
1/4 cup Dijon mustard
2 shallots, diced
1 clove garlic, minced
1 teaspoon cayenne pepper

Marinade
1/4 cup olive oil
3/4 cup red wine
1 teaspoon cracked black pepper
2 cloves garlic, minced
1/2 teaspoon habañero pepper sauce
pinch rosemary, thyme and salt

Sauce
5 whole garlic cloves
2 tablespoons white sugar
3/4 cup vegetable stock
3/4 cup beef stock

Steveston Seafood House
3951 Moncton Street
Steveston, BC
(604) 271-5252

Since 1978
STEVESTON
SEAFOOD HOUSE

Steveston Seafood House, set in traditional Steveston Village, has become internationally and locally known for fine seafood dining since 1978. Appropriately located near the Fraser River and the fishing docks, the Steveston Seafood House continues to earn its reputation as "that great little seafood place in Richmond." The decor is funky, with a nautical motif featuring overhead nets, glass floats, and corny seashell knickknacks. Seafood, simply prepared and generously served on large fish-shaped plates, delivers all it promises. We recommend any of the house specialties—even ones with names like Jonathan Livingston Seafood (a mixed seafood platter)—but you shouldn't overlook simple dishes such as the juicy pan-fried halibut with lemon butter.

A succulent blend of a West Coast fisherman's catch.

Chef's Seafood Special

In sauté pan, place 2 tablespoons clarified butter, heat pan until hot. Squeeze half lemon onto halibut and salt and pepper. Dredge halibut in flour. Place halibut in hot sauté pan until lightly brown, turn over and repeat. Finish cooking halibut in 400 degree oven, approximately 10 minutes.

In a saucepan add white wine, whole butter, fresh dill, minced garlic and mussels. Place pan on high heat and cover. Mussels are done when fully opened. In a sauté pan place remaining clarified butter and heat pan until hot. Add red onion, lemon juice from half a lemon, capers, prawns and scallops that have been dredged in flour. Reduce to medium heat and cook until prawns change colour, and scallops turn opaque.

Place mussels in a shallow bowl. Remove halibut from oven and place on large dish, top with prawns, scallops, capers and red onion; sauté. Serve with rice and vegetables, and garnish with fresh dill and a lemon crown.

1/4 cup capers

1 cup white wine

1 teaspoon minced fresh dill

1 tablespoon minced garlic

2 lemons

1 cup flour

salt and pepper

8 ounces halibut filet

3 scallops

3 black tiger prawns

2 tablespoons whole butter

1/4 cup clarified butter

2 cups mussels

1/4 cup red onions, julienned

48

La Bodega
Restaurante & Tapa-Bar — SINCE 1971

La Bodega
1277 Howe Street
Vancouver, BC
(604) 684-8814
(604) 684-8815

Step inside "La Bodega" and you will find a delightful little corner of Spain in the middle of Downtown Vancouver. For the last 27 years, Jose and Paco have been working hard at serving traditional Spanish cuisine and hospitality. A menu featuring tasty "Tapas" and a selection of entrees including chicken, lamb, beef, fish and vegetarian plates will transport you to the very heart of Spain. The featured "Paella" is without a doubt the best known dish. A savoury blend of saffron and rice with an adventurous mix of pork, mussels, clams, chicken and prawns keeps diners coming back after so many years. A jug of Sangria, a bottle of light red wine or a crisp, fruity white wine would complement this dish, allowing the mixture of flavours to be enjoyed independently. Say "Si" and join the fun as one of Vancouver's longest operating restaurants invites you to be their guest.

A Gastronomical "Babel", but a delightful confusion.

Paella

Season the chicken with salt and pepper, then brown it in a "paellera" or large frying pan; set aside. In the same "paellera" add veal or pork, onion, garlic, green pepper and tomatoes. Season mixture and keep stirring until all appears cooked to your taste. Stir in paprika, saffron and rice; add stock and bring to a boil. Arrange chicken, prawns, clams and mussels on the rice. Lower heat and cook until stock is almost gone. Add green peas and strips of red pimientos. Finish cooking in hot oven. Decorate with lemon wedges. Serves 6 to 8.

1/4 cup olive oil

1 small piece chicken per person

1/2 pound veal or pork, cubed

1/2 medium onion chopped

2 cloves garlic, finely chopped

1 medium green pepper, chopped

3 tomatoes, seeded and chopped

1 teaspoon mild paprika

pinch saffron

salt and pepper

3 cups converted rice

8 cups chicken stock

18 small hard shell clams

18 fresh mussels

18 medium prawns

1 cup shelled green peas

2 canned red pimientos

2 lemons

PALIOTTI'S
Ristorante Italiano

Paliotti's Ristorante Italiano
12018 Edge Street
Maple Ridge, BC
(604) 463-8926

To taste Italian cuisine as good or better than Italy, one no longer needs to purchase an airline ticket. In addition to a wide variety of homemade pasta, Paliotti Restaurant features fresh veal, lamb, chicken, fish and salads. The featured recipe, Fettuccini Paliotti, is renowned by connoisseurs of Italian cooking throughout Vancouver and the Lower Mainland. This blend of bacon, mushrooms, onions and garlic has customers returning time and time again. Paliotti's Restaurant is a short drive to Maple Ridge. Situated on the corner of Dewdney Trunk Road and Edge Street, it is just east of the "Beast," Maple Ridge's aluminum horse.

...bacon, mushrooms, onions and garlic simmered with pasta, cream and parmesan cheese.

Fettuccini Paliotti

Using a large pan (preferably Teflon), fry bacon or ham until cooked. Add onions and cook to transparency. Add mushrooms, garlic and butter and cook until tender over medium heat. Add white wine (optional) and cream, then simmer until sauce starts to bubble. Add cooked fettuccini and toss while sauce is simmering. Add parmesan cheese. Your pasta dish should be moist but not over sauced. Pour onto pasta platter and serve immediately. For a seafood version, just add shrimp or prawns.

1 cup bacon or ham, diced 1/2 inch width

1/2 cup onion, chopped

2 cups mushrooms, sliced

1/8 to 1/4 cup of garlic, peeled and sliced to taste

1/4 cup butter

1/4 cup white wine (optional)

1/2 quart whipping cream 32 to 36 percent

1/2 cup parmesan cheese, imported

500 grams fettuccini, cooked

salt and pepper to taste

52

MONK McQUEENS
Fresh Seafood & Oyster Bar

McQueens Upstairs
601 Stamps Landing
Vancouver, BC
(604) 877-1351

A seafood lover's paradise. Located on a picturesque setting over the waters of False Creek's south shore, McQueens Upstairs is a vibrant spot where patio dining during the summer months has been taken to new heights. Recipient of "People's Choice of Best Patio" 12 years running, McQueens Upstairs offers an intimate evening of refined menu and ambiance. Where the jazz piano and small dance floor—along with Vancouver's skyline—can close romantically about your candlelit table, McQueens Upstairs offers culinary delights including Fresh Dungeness Crab Salad, Ginger Salmon, Smoked Alaskan Black Cod, Grilled Ahi Tuna au Poivre, Roasted Rack of Lamb and Grilled Alberta Filet Mignon. McQueens' wine list offers a more extensive selection for the connoisseur. Reservations are recommended. McQueens is involved with the following charities: Boys and Girls Club of Greater Vancouver; Vancouver Children's Hospital; Orca Bay Charitable Foundation; Vancouver Food Bank; Syd Vernon Charitable Foundation.

*succulent shellfish and traditional pasta,
tossed in flavourful light herb cream sauce.*

Pappardelle Pasta

Heat the olive oil in a large skillet. When oil is hot, add the clams and sauté them for about 30 seconds over medium-high heat. Add the leeks, garlic and tiger prawns. Continue to sauté for another 30 seconds. Add the cream and then reduce by 1/3—about 30 seconds. Add the pasta and cook until the cream thickens, about 1 minute. Season with salt and pepper to taste. Transfer to serving plates when the clams and mussels are open and pasta is hot. Top with the julienne of smoked salmon lox. Serve and Enjoy!

4 fresh tiger prawns, peeled and deveined

6 fresh mussels, debearded and scrubbed

6 fresh local clams

1 ounce fresh smoked salmon lox

1/4 cup leeks, julienned

1 teaspoon fresh garlic, minced

2 ounces cream

1 ounce cooked fresh pappardelle pasta

1 ounce olive oil

pinch salt and pepper

The Old Country Inn

Old Country Inn
20598 Fraser Highway
Langley, BC
(604) 534-8696

The Old Country Inn is famous in the Lower Mainland for providing culinary delights with a European flavour and an atmosphere of casual comfort and elegance. The menu exemplifies the finest tradition of European cuisine, with appetizers including favourites like Escargots Bourguinonne, Prawns Provencales, Oysters Rockefeller and Hungarian Goulasch Soup. Entrees include some of the finest seafood dishes, succulent schnitzels, roast duckling, chateaubriand and rack of lamb, supplemented by innovative items like pastas and vegetarian dishes to reflect changing trends. All desserts are irresistible and homemade. Choose from a Black Forest Torte, chocolate confections, cheesecakes or the ultimate indulgence, Crepes Suzettes, prepared and flambéed at your table. All selections are complemented by an extensive wine list featuring fine European and Canadian wines. Patrons will be surprised and delighted by the restaurant's elegant charm and atmosphere coupled with superior service and personal attention.

Roasted Rack of Spring Lamb with a Minted Demi-Glace.

Rack of Lamb

Season a well trimmed and "Frenched" seven-rib rack of lamb with salt, minced garlic and freshly ground black pepper. Rub the top with prepared Dijon mustard and place into a heavy skillet. Roast in the oven for 35 minutes to a medium point. Remove from the skillet and keep warm.

On the top of the stove, sauté 1 tablespoon of finely chopped onions or eschalottes until transparent. Drain lamb fat off and add 2 ounces of prepared mint sauce. Reduce by gently simmering by half. Add 4 ounces of Demi-Glace (brown red wine sauce) and continue to simmer. Cut the rack into individual chops. Pour sauce onto hot dinner plate and place chops on top of the sauce in a fan design. Surround the meat with assorted colourful vegetables and potatoes. Serve.

Wines that complement this dish are Cabernet Sauvignon, Merlot, Beaujolais or Pinot Noir.

rack of lamb (seven rib)

1 to 2 cloves fresh garlic, minced

2 teaspoons Dijon mustard

1 tablespoon eschalottes or onions, finely chopped

2 ounces prepared mint sauce

4 ounces demi-glace (brown red wine sauce)

56

L'Arena Ristorante
300 West Georgia St.
Vancouver, BC
(604) 687-5434

Tucked into Library Square, L'Arena has become a new favourite among locals. Conveniently located in the heart of the sports and entertainment district, L'Arena is Vancouver's premier event dinner house—before or after the event. Featuring Vancouver's best Italian brunch buffet, as well as a menu that blends classical Italian dishes with flavours from the Far East and Europe, the service is very friendly (they anticipate and expect the theatre crowd), and the ambiance is relaxed so you don't have to worry about missing the curtain call. An excellent array of wines has earned L'Arena the honour of a 1998 Wine Spectator Award of Excellence. The featured dish, chicken saltimbocca, is a L'Arena specialty, but veal can be substituted to make this dish in its original form.

Chicken with prosciutto in a sage butter cream sauce

Chicken Saltimbocca

Using a meat tenderizer, pound the chicken breasts until 1/4 inch thick. Place three sage leaves on each chicken breast and then place one slice prosciutto on top. Using a toothpick, fasten the chicken breast and the prosciutto together so it does not fall apart while cooking.

Melt the butter in a saucepan over medium-high heat. When the butter has melted, make sure the pan is hot and add the chicken; cook for about two minutes; deglaze the pan with the white wine and let reduce by half; turn chicken over and cook for about one minute. Remove the chicken and keep warm.

Return pan to the stove, then add the whipping cream. Bring to a boil and reduce until sauce thickens. Pour the sauce over the chicken and serve immediately with your choice of accompaniments.

4   4 ounce skinless chicken breasts

4 ounces prosciutto

12 sage leaves

2 ounces butter

2 ounces white wine

4 ounces heavy whipping cream

salt and pepper to taste

Romano's Macaroni Grill

1523 Davie Street
Vancouver, BC
(604) 689-4334

Discover why Italians are so passionate about their food at Romano's Macaroni Grill. Executive Chef Alex Rotherham prepares classic Italian dishes that incorporate the freshest ingredients including chicken, seafood, pasta and pizzas. Our Scallopini di Pollo is a simple chicken dish that uses the blending of such exotic ingredients as pancetta, capers, and artichoke hearts to create a truly magnificent flavour. A fine Chardonnay would be the perfect complement for this dish, enhancing the flavours already present. Romano's Macaroni Grill is located in Gabriola Mansion, a heritage building. Open for lunch and dinner with several rooms that make it ideal for everything from a quick bite, to a large dinner party or a luncheon. Valet parking is available during dinner.

Tender pan-fried chicken in a rich lemon butter sauce on vermicelli

Scallopini di Pollo

Cut chicken breasts into 2 ounce pieces. Dredge in flour to provide a light coating. Preheat a large frying pan and add olive oil. Add chicken breasts and sauté until half cooked then turn over. In a second pan, heat olive oil and add mushrooms, capers, pancetta and minced garlic. Sauté for about 2 minutes. Add heavy cream, lemon juice and white wine. Bring to a simmer. Cook vermicelli in a pot of boiling water. Follow instructions on product package. When cooked, strain, toss in olive oil and serve in a bowl, garnished with parsley. Melt butter into sauce. Add cooked chicken to plate of vermicelli. Pour sauce over chicken, garnish with parsley and serve.

2 pounds boneless chicken breasts

1/2 pound sliced mushrooms

1/4 cup white flour

2 fluid ounces olive oil

8 artichoke hearts, quartered

1 ounce capers

4 ounces pancetta, fried and crumbled

1 fluid ounce lemon juice

1 fluid ounce white wine

2 fluid ounces heavy cream

1/4 ounce minced garlic

5 ounces unsalted butter

1 pound dried vermicelli

1 teaspoon parsley

Roasted Pheasant

La Toque Blanche
4368 Marine Drive
West Vancouver, BC
(604) 926-1006

John Carlo Felicella, owner, has been a life-long North Shore resident born and raised in West Vancouver. After completing the Culinary Arts Program, John Carlo moved on to be sous-chef and executive chef at some of Vancouver's finest hotels and resorts. Currently, he is a member of Culinary Team B. C. and his most recent achievement was a gold medal at the prestigious Culinary Olympics in Berlin, Germany in 1996. La Toque Blanche offers a unique combination of contemporary West Coast and classical cuisine with special attention to the balance of presentation and flavour. In addition to a formal dining room, La Toque Blanche offers full-service catering for any event, from simple to formal. Voted one of North Shore's Best, come and see what makes La Toque Blanche West Vancouver's most intimate hideaway.

Delectable pheasant roasted and served with pumpkin stew

Over medium heat, sauté shallots and sugar in butter until caramelization begins. Add pumpkin and nutmeg; continue to cook for 1 minute. Add chicken stock and zest; simmer until pumpkin starts to break down. Season to taste and set aside.

Rub pepper, oil and sage on pheasant, season with salt. Over medium heat, lightly brown breasts in butter; put into 375 degree oven for 2 minutes. When slightly firm to touch, remove from pan and set aside to rest for 10 minutes. In pheasant roasting pan, sauté shallots, orange and star anise in butter at medium heat until caramelized. Splash with brandy and slightly reduce. Add beef jus and reduce by half. Strain through fine sieve and adjust seasoning. Place pheasant on the pumpkin stew, spoon brandy sauce around and on pheasant. Accompany with asparagus and serve.

50 grams unsalted butter

754 grams shallots, finely minced

10 grams sugar

400 grams pumpkin, diced

2 grams fresh nutmeg, ground

100 milliliters pheasant or chicken stock

zest of 2 oranges

salt and cracked pepper to taste

4 pheasant breasts

fresh sage, julienned

50 milliliters canola oil

30 grams unsalted butter

1 drop star anise essence

orange segments from 2 oranges

20 grams unsalted butter

50 grams shallots, finely minced

50 milliliters brandy

300 milliliters rich beef jus

Tojo's Rainbow Roll

Tojo's Japanese Restaurant
#202-777 West Broadway Avenue
Vancouver, BC
(604) 872-8050

Master Sushi Chef Hidekazu Tojo (Tojo-San) has five years of Master Sushi Chef training in Osaka, Japan. Over the last 30 years, he has become internationally well known for his distinct brand of Japanese food. Since his opening in 1988, he has been creating traditional Japanese dishes—full of wonderful, natural flavours—with his own brilliant, creative methods. He uses only the freshest of ingredients and pays attention to every detail. Even though the dining room has a breathtaking view of False Creek, downtown Vancouver and the North Shore, repeat customers vie for a spot at the 10-seat open sushi bar. Winner of countless "Best Japanese" and "Best Seafood" awards, the truly superb cuisine is what keeps his customers so loyal.

Tojo's world-famous rainbow roll wrapped in salmon, tuna and red snapper

Cover both sides of bamboo rolling mat with plastic wrap. Cut 1 rectangular sheet of nori in half. Place half-sheet, shiny side down. With dampened fingers, spread sushi rice in even layer over nori, handling lightly. Flip sheet over, back onto bamboo mat (rice facing down and nori facing up). Spread a thin band of wasabi across centre of nori. Cover wasabi with crabmeat and cucumber strips. Roll by grasping mat by front edge, rolling firmly to close ingredients in centre. Roll again to close completely. Set aside.

To produce outside "rainbow striped" layer, arrange prepared fish and tamago strips in a diagonal fashion on rolling mat, repeating in this order, salmon, sprouts, tuna, tamago, red snapper. Repeat to length of roll. Place "inside-out" roll onto strips, rice-side down. Roll to enclose. Cover with plastic wrap, tube fashion. Cut into 6 inch pieces. Serve with gari as garnish.

* 2 sheets nori (dried laver seaweed)

* prepared wasabi (Japanese green horseradish)

1 cup cucumber strips, julienned

1/2 cup fresh lump crabmeat

Daikon sprouts, blanched

1/4 inch by 2 inch strips: fresh salmon, tuna, red snapper, tamago (egg crêpe)

* Gari (pickled ginger)

* prepared sushi rice (Japanese short-grain rice marinated in Japanese rice vinegar, kelp, sugar and salt)

*These items may be purchased at Asian markets.

64

Flaming Prawns

**The Fish House
in Stanley Park**
8901 Stanley Park Dr.
Vancouver, BC
(604) 681-7275

Critics voted "Best Seafood Restaurant" in Vancouver for 1996 and 1997. We invite you to enjoy our three handsome rooms in a charming house overlooking putting greens, tennis courts and English Bay. Here seafood rules (salmon, seabass, shellfish of all kinds) - everything you would expect and some things you wouldn't. Also, pasta and wood-oven specialties are prepared by renowned Executive Chef Karen Barnaby. Try our Grilled West Coast Salmon with Maple Glaze or our signature Grilled Ahi Tuna Steak "Diane" complimented by our Award winning Wine list.

You can visit Lord Stanley's Oyster Bar inside or relax on our umbrella'd sunny patios overlooking the park. Take a one hour vacation away from your busy day. In addition, we offer a private dining room in our unique and famous wine cellar. Reservations are recommended.

A tempting and exciting dish of prawns and sweet bell peppers flambéed in ouzo

In a large frying pan, heat olive oil over high heat. Add garlic, and when sizzling, add prawns and stir fry until pink. Add peppers and tomatoes and stir-fry until the prawns are cooked through. Heat heavy cast iron pan over high heat. Have a heavy wooden board available to place pan on when ready to flame prawns. Ouzo and lemon should be on the board. Add feta and basil to prawns and stir to combine. Transfer prawns to one side of pan and place pan on the board. Carry the board to the table and advise everyone to stay well back. Pour the ouzo into the empty side of the pan and ignite immediately with a long match. Squeeze the lemon over the prawns to douse the flames, then give the prawns a stir. If pyrotechnics are not your style, just add the ouzo to the prawns after they have finished cooking. This, however, lacks drama. Serve with pasta, rice or bread to mop up the juices.

*Used by permission of Whitecap Books

1 tablespoon olive oil

1 teaspoon garlic, minced

24 large prawns, peeled and deveined

1/2 cup roasted sweet red peppers, coarsely chopped

1/2 cup canned Italian plum tomatoes, drained, coarsely chopped

1/2 cup crumbled feta cheese

1/4 cup fresh basil leaves

1 ounce ouzo

1/2 lemon, seeds removed

Geschnetzeltes Mit Roesti

**Tudor Room
at The Park Royal Hotel**
540 Clyde Avenue
West Vancouver, BC
(604) 926-5511

It is not uncommon to find innkeeper Mario Corsi by the canopied entranceway of the Park Royal Hotel greeting longtime patrons. His voice, rich and resonant, is unmistakable. His is a genuine welcome. Mario's small hotel, particularly the Tudor Room, has long been a place for Vancouver's business people to gather and talk. The dining room is private and the tables are widely spaced; important for closing those important deals. The service is discreet and the setting cannot be matched anywhere in the city. Golf-green lawns have been meticulously groomed and roses bloom effortlessly by the entrance. Rhododendrons and azaleas flower in the beautiful garden, nestled beside the river. Fresh herbs, particularly basil, are tucked between the rows. Paradise in West Vancouver.

A delicious veal dish in a white wine cream sauce served with Roesti.

Heat skillet until very hot. Add oil, and sauté meat quickly until brown. Stir in mushrooms, onion and butter. Season lightly with salt and pepper. Dust with flour; continue to sauté for one or two minutes. Stirring constantly, pour in wine and cream. Return to boil, reduce temperature and simmer for two or three minutes.

For Roesti, peel potatoes and slowly grate on coarse side of grater. The shreds should be long. Heat non-stick skillet over medium high heat. Add butter and when bubbling subsides, add potato, salt and pepper. Cover and sauté until underside is golden brown. Loosen edges and flip entire potato cake. Sauté until second side is browned. Serve immediately.

2 tablespoons olive oil

1 pound veal tenderloin, thinly sliced

8 ounces fresh mushrooms, sliced

1 small onion, diced

1/4 cup butter

salt and freshly ground pepper to taste

1 tablespoon all purpose flour

1/2 cup dry white wine

1 cup table cream (18 percent)

Roesti or hot buttered noodles

<u>Roesti</u>

4 cooked, unpeeled potatoes (must be refrigerated for 2 to 3 days prior)

1 tablespoon butter

salt and freshly ground pepper to taste

Linguini con Vongole

Caffe de Medici
1025 Robson St.
Vancouver, BC
(604) 669-9322
email: medici@settingsun.com
www.settingsun.com/medici

"As you enter Caffe de Medici, you are immediately made to feel like a favourite guest. The high molded ceilings, serene portraits of the fifteenth-century Medici family, chairs and drapery in Renaissance green against crisp white table linen, and walls the colour of zabaglione create a lightly palatial feeling; diplomatic waiters appear pleased to be look after your needs. Businesslike by day, romantic by night, the mood changes, but the quality of the Northern Italian food does not. Order the beautiful antipasto; a bright collage of marinated eggplant, artichoke hearts, peppers, olives, squid and Italian cold meats. Pasta dishes are flat-out magnifico—a light chewy plateful of tortellini alla panna arrives so rich with cheese you'll never order any of the others. Although it's mainly a Florentine restaurant, we've also sampled a fine Roman-style rack of lamb."

- Kasey Wilson and Stephanie Irving, authors of "Vancouver's Best Places."

In a large pot, bring water to a rapid boil. Add the linguini slowly, gradually bending it around the inside of the pot as it softens. Stir continuously. Perfect pasta should be slightly firm in the centre. Pour the cooked linguini into a colander and set in the sink. In a large heavy saucepan over medium heat, sauté crushed garlic in the olive oil, stir constantly, being sure not to burn the garlic. Add freshly washed clams with white wine and steam until clams open. Add chilies and parsley. Add pasta and finish with butter. Salt and pepper to taste and then enjoy!

250 milliliters cooked linguine

700 grams fresh clams

1 clove garlic, crushed

30 milliliters olive oil

chilies to taste

200 milliliters white wine

30 milliliters chopped parsley

30 milliliters sweet butter

salt and pepper

Honey & Ginger Beef

Kirin Mandarin Restaurant

麒麟川菜館

Kirin Mandarin Restaurant
1166 Alberni Street
(Downtown) Vancouver, BC
(604) 682-8833

The Kirin Mandarin Restaurant, named after the Chinese mythological dragon of good omen, has much more than good luck on its side. Executive chef Gary Chow is a master of Chinese cooking. Just one taste of his authentic Northern Chinese cuisine and you will see. Specialties include Peking Duck, Deep-fried Smoked Duck, Kung Pao Style Lobster, Pink Swimming Scallops, Rock Salt and Pepper Prawns, Beggar's Chicken and Dim Sum. Any choice from the menu is the right choice. With elegant surroundings tastefully decorated in a Mandarin motif—you'd think you were in China once you walk through the doors!

"Tai chi mut"—"it tastes like honey",
we suggest steamed buns with this dish.

Slice beef paper thin, across the grain. Marinate 15 minutes with hoisin sauce and cornstarch. Heat 300 milliliters oil in wok to 360 degrees Fahrenheit. Deep fry marinated beef 1 minute, lift out at once with a strainer and drain. Set aside. Discard oil, wipe wok clean and return 15 milliliters oil to wok and heat. Have ready combined garlic, ginger and scallion, and stir fry 1 minute. Add honey and soya sauce, cook 15 seconds and return drained beef to wok. Stir fry 1 minute until beef is glazed. Serve on a platter, garnished with sprigs of Chinese parsley. Accompany with warm steamed buns.

250 grams beef tenderloin

60 milliliters hoisin sauce

5 milliliters cornstarch

300 milliliters vegetable oil

15 milliliters vegetable oil

3 cloves garlic, minced

4 thin slices ginger, minced

1 scallion, white only, cut into thin shreds

30 milliliters honey

30 milliliters dark soya sauce

fresh Chinese parsley sprigs

72

Pasta Made Perfect

The Water St. Cafe
300 Water St.
Vancouver, BC
(604) 689-2832

A Gastown cornerstone since 1988, The Water St. Cafe overlooks Gastown's cobbled streets and the world-famous steam clock. The high ceilings and large windows make for a bright and casual atmosphere. The summer sidewalk patio is an ideal place for people watching while dining in one of Vancouver's best neighbourhood restaurants. Fresh seafoods, creative pastas, daily fresh features and more are prepared with an attention to detail and imagination for you to enjoy. The Water St. Cafe, what every small restaurant ought to be: a commitment to quality food, value and service that keeps customers coming back again and again. Owner Dominique Sabatino invites you to try "Pasta Made Perfect," made this way because penne is an Italian classic; and the plum tomatoes and cracked red chilies complement the spiced Italian sausage which is seared in extra virgin olive oil with a blend of the finest herbs and garlic. Open daily from 11:30 a.m. till late, located across the street from the steam clock. Two private rooms are also available for parties of 10 to 40.

Penne with Italian sausage, plum tomatoes, red chilies, extra virgin olive oil

In a food processor, chop medium-fine both tins of roma tomatoes in juice. In a large pan heat 2 tablespoons of olive oil. Sauté onion, carrot and celery. Add the above tomato mixture, the dried portion of basil, 1 tablespoon fresh basil, oregano, thyme, black pepper and salt to taste. Simmer for approximately 30 minutes or until quantity is reduced by 1/3. In another large pan, heat the remaining olive oil. Sear sausage meat until golden brown. Add and sauté garlic, shallot, fresh roma tomato, parsley and remaining basil. Add simmered tomato sauce and simmer until reduced by 1/3. Toss together with penne cooked al dente and serve.

2 tablespoons onion, finely minced

2 tablespoons carrot, finely minced

2 tablespoons celery, finely minced

4 tablespoons olive oil

2 20 ounce cans whole roma tomatoes, finely chopped

pinch dry oregano

pinch dried thyme

1 teaspoon dry basil

black pepper and salt to taste

3 tablespoons fresh basil leaves

1 1/4 pounds medium spicy sausage

1 clove garlic, minced

1 shallot, finely chopped

1 cup fresh roma tomato, 1/4 inch dice

2 tablespoons fresh parsley

cracked red chilies to taste

400 grams raw weight penne pasta

Tea Smoked Cedar Plank Salmon

**Joe Fortes
Seafood & Chop House**
777 Thurlow Street
Vancouver, BC
(604) 669-1940

Vancouver's Best Oyster Bar & Grill with live piano and a bustling social atmosphere. Serving the freshest seafood, complemented by an award-winning wine list. Voted "Most Memorable Meal 1996" by Where Magazine. Joe's Grill on the Roof offers a rooftop patio for summer outdoor dining overlooking the bustling city below.

Tea-smoked cedar planked salmon is a Joe Fortes Seafood & Chop House signature dish. The salmon is lightly smoked with chamomile tea, offering a unique flavour. Serve with organic greens and sautéed vegetables. This dish is wonderful when accompanied by a glass of Kanke Chardonnay.

salmon lightly smoked with chamomile tea

Mix lemon grass, garlic, ginger, shallots, sesame oil, soya sauce, rosemary and maple syrup in a bowl. Marinate the salmon in the mixture for 15 minutes. Remove salmon from the marinade and place on a dry cloth. Place the salmon on a hotel pan and then in a smoker for 15 minutes. *It is important to add tea to the smoking chips for flavour. Remove the salmon from smoker and season with salt and pepper to taste. Then place on a pre-soaked cedar plank and place in the oven at 375 degrees for 7 minutes. Can be served with organic greens and sautéed vegetables.

Recommended wine: Chardonnay

2 salmon steaks

chamomile tea

Salmon Marinade

2 teaspoons chopped lemon grass

2 teaspoons garlic

2 teaspoons ginger

2 teaspoons shallots

1 cup sesame oil

1/4 cup soya sauce

1 cup chopped rosemary

2 teaspoons maple syrup

salt and cracked pepper to taste

Steak Tartare

hy's ENCORE

A "CHARCOAL BROIL" SPECIALTY HOUSE

Hy's Encore
637 Hornby Street
Vancouver, BC
(604) 683-7671

Hy's Encore, Vancouver's renowned steak house for the past 35 years, is loaded with history and tradition. A collection of antiques, rich velvet and dark wood-paneled rooms radiate a decor which is both comfortable and elegant. Dominating the room—where diners often request window seats—a giant window allows guests to view chefs grilling perfectly aged charcoal steaks. Manager Willem Liekens and Chef Wilson Lo reflect Hy's philosophy: "large portions to keep the customer happy and content so they will always come back for more." Hy's signature feature of being consistent has earned its reputation of being not only Canada's oldest, but premier, steak house in the country.

Steak Tartare for two

Grind garlic into bottom of large salad bowl. Gently add chopped filet, capers, onion, paprika, ketchup and brandy. Season well with Hy's Seasoning Salt and freshly ground pepper. Add egg yolk and blend ingredients together. On a cold serving plate, form the mixture into a mound. Garnish with tomato and lettuce slices, cross with anchovy filets and serve with slices of melba toast.

3 1/2 ounce lean filet mignon, ask butcher to prepare trimmed, finely chopped

2 teaspoons whole capers

2 teaspoons onion, finely chopped

1/2 teaspoon onion, finely chopped

1/2 teaspoon paprika

1 clove garlic

1 teaspoon tomato ketchup

1 whole egg yolk

1 teaspoon brandy

Hy's Seasoning Salt, to taste

freshly ground pepper, to taste

Garnish

2 fillets anchovies, thinly sliced

tomato slices, lettuce leaf

Tabasco sauce

melba toast or thinly sliced baguette

Vegetarian Steam Baskets

Galleries on the Plateau
3251 Plateau Boulevard
Coquitlam, BC
(604) 552-5151

Exquisite fusion cuisine—blending masterpieces from the West Coast with delights from around the Pacific—are the hallmarks of Galleries' chefs. Add exceptional service, charming decor, a wood-burning fireplace, breathtaking views of Mount Baker and the surrounding mountains, and Galleries gives new meaning to breakfast, lunch and dinner, making them special experiences to be savored forever. Dinner might consist of Baked Northwest Oysters, to be followed by a Singapore Salad, Rack of Lamb and a Warm Apple Filo Tower. Galleries also features an Oyster Bar, and a carefully selected wine list specializing in wines from around the Pacific Rim and beyond. Galleries on the Plateau, one of Coquitlam's newest restaurants, offers an upscale dining experience in a casual atmosphere. Reservations recommended on weekends.

Vegetarian steam baskets with marinated noodles for two.

Using 2 10 inch round bamboo steam baskets with lids, line baskets with lettuce and kale, leaving spaces for the steam to pass through. In a bowl, mix cooked chow mein noodles with the sesame seeds, rice vinegar, sesame oil and cilantro. Pile marinated noodles in the center of lettuce- lined baskets. Arrange vegetables and tofu in a decorative manner around the noodles. Cover with steam basket lids. Using pots that the steam baskets can fit into, fill with one inch of water and bring to a boil. Place baskets into the pots and steam for approximately 10 minutes, depending on how crisp you like your vegetables. Place the steam baskets on large plates and serve with wasabi, soya sauce and pickled ginger.

4 cups cooked chow mein noodles

2 tablespoons black and white sesame seeds

4 tablespoons seasoned rice vinegar

4 tablespoons sesame oil

2 tablespoons fresh cilantro, chopped

4 pieces tofu, medium to firm

6 carrot slices

6 mushrooms

6 asparagus

2 each broccoli and cauliflower florets

2 slices each red, yellow and green bell peppers

2 green onions

lettuce and kale

Grilled Salmon Burrito

Las Margaritas
1999 West 4th Avenue
Vancouver, BC
(604) 734-7117
www.lasmargaritas.com

Las Margaritas, a popular Mexican eatery for the last 17 years in Vancouver's trendy Kitsilano area, has been transformed by new owner Dan Rodriguez, who bought the establishment 4 years ago and has truly put his name on it. Voted People's Choice "Best Mexican" in 1997, Las Margaritas combines the influences of interior Mexico, the Baja Peninsula and Southern California. Traditional dishes include a wide range of enchiladas, fajitas and burritos. House specialties include our grilled Salmon Burrito and Pollo Loco (half chicken marinated in an achiote sauce, baked, then grilled). Enjoy one of our award-winning Margaritas in our beautiful walled-in patio just around the corner from Fourth Avenue's eclectic shopping district. Las Margaritas also serves Mexican Brunch on Saturdays and Sundays.

Flour tortilla filled with cilantro-pesto marinated salmon, black beans & cheese

Purée marinade ingredients in food processor. Pour mixture into a shallow pan. Roll salmon pieces in the mixture until all sides are coated. Cover and refrigerate for 2 hours.

To make sauce, preheat heavy bottomed saucepan to medium-high. Add oil, garlic, jalapeño and onion; sauté until slightly browned. Add water, plum tomatoes, grilled tomatoes, chilies, cream, oregano and salt. Bring to a boil; continue to cook on medium-low heat until mixture reduces by half and develops a syrupy consistency. Remove from heat. Pureée in food processor until smooth, return to pan and simmer for 5 to 10 minutes. Sauce should be thick enough to coat the back of a metal spoon.

Preheat char-grill to medium, grill salmon for 10 to 11 minutes; about 2 minutes on each side, brushing with remaining marinade after each turn.

Roll each piece of grilled salmon into a tortilla with 1/4 ounce of feta, 1 ounce black beans and 1 ounce chipotle sauce. Pour 3 ounces of chipotle sauce and crumble 1/2 ounce feta along the top of each burrito and place under broiler until cheese is slightly browned. Garnish with chopped green onions, serve with rice and black beans.

4 2 ounce red spring salmon filets, boneless, skinless
3 ounces feta cheese
6 ounces black beans, cooked
4 8 inch flour tortillas

Marinade
5 ounces cilantro leaves
3/4 ounce toasted almonds
1/2 ounce garlic cloves, peeled
1 jalapeño pepper
2 cups olive oil

Chipotle Cream Sauce
1 ounce whole garlic cloves
1 jalapeño pepper
1 teaspoon canned chipotle chilies
11 ounces peeled white onion, chopped
6 ounces fresh tomatoes, grilled
1/4 liter water
1/4 liter canned plum tomatoes
1/2 liter 33 percent cream
1/4 teaspoon oregano
1/4 teaspoon salt
3 tablespoons olive oil

Crostini alla Romana

For 8 years, Zefferelli's has been one of the favourites for Vancouverites when it comes to enjoying casual Italian cooking. Nestled in the heart of Robson Street, this second-floor spaghetti joint creates a warm, simple and comfortable space from where Executive Chef Alberto Lemmo offers innovative dishes that lie within everyone's comfort zone. This feature recipe can be enjoyed as both an appetizer or combined with a favorite starch and vegetable as an entree. To get the full culinary effect of this dish, open a bottle of Valpolicella and let the flavors go wild. Listed by Jorgen Gothe as one of the top five chicken liver dishes in Vancouver. Come by and see for yourself. Reservations are highly recommended.

Zefferelli's

Zefferelli's
1136 Robson Street
Vancouver, BC
(604) 687-0655

A savoury blend of chicken livers, fresh sage and sherry

In a large frying pan heat vegetable oil on medium to high heat. Add bread slices to oil until golden brown. Remove bread and place on paper towel. In the same pan, add onions, chicken livers and garlic. On medium heat, sauté mixture until desired doneness. Remove from heat. Add sage, sherry and season with salt and pepper. Place bread on serving plate and top each slice with equal amounts of the liver and sauce mixture. Garnish with fresh chopped sage.

4 slices Italian bread

3 fluid ounces vegetable oil

800 grams chicken livers, quartered

3 fluid ounces onion, finely chopped

1 teaspoon garlic, finely chopped

8 leaves fresh sage

4 fluid ounces medium sherry

salt and pepper to taste

84

Mushroom Strudel

HERONS

WATERFRONT CENTRE HOTEL
CANADIAN PACIFIC
HOTELS

Herons
900 Canada Place Way
Vancouver, BC
(604) 691-1818

Just off the lobby at Waterfront Centre Hotel, Herons Restaurant & Lounge features two stories of floor-to-ceiling windows, allowing a panoramic harbour view of the snow-capped North Shore mountains glistening in the sun, tree-lined Stanley Park and cruise ships gliding into shore. Herons Restaurant offers cuisine with a West Coast flair reflecting local and regional specialties of the Pacific Rim. Herons' open kitchen reveals the scenery with an à la carte menu, breakfast and lunch buffets, dinner and a daily fresh sheet providing a variety of seasonal flavours. From the planting of the seeds to the last garnish on the plate, Chef Nagata enjoys creating a bouquet of herbal delights, fresh from the hotel's 2100-square-foot herb garden on the hotel's third floor terrace. Fresh basil, thyme, lemon-grass thyme, parsley, Italian flat parsley, sage, chives and lavender are just a few of the herbs and edible flowers used in his recipes and fresh garnishings.

Fennel and thyme-crusted exotic mushroom strudel....

Strudel: Sauté spinach, garlic, shallots with two tablespoons of walnut oil on medium heat for approximately 20 seconds and hold at room temperature. Sauté mushrooms in 2 tablespoons walnut oil on medium-high heat for 30 seconds and add 1/2 cup vermouth and cook for another 1 1/2 minutes at room temperature. Lay out a sheet of phyllo dough, lightly brush with remaining olive oil. Sprinkle with fennel seeds and thyme. Fold in half, add 1/4 of the spinach, 1/4 of the mushrooms and a piece of feta cheese on top. Fold the sides over and roll until entire sheet is rolled up. Bake at 375 degrees for 8 to 12 minutes until golden brown. Cut in 3 and serve with the leek, garlic and vermouth sauce.

Sauce: Strain, season and purée leeks and garlic. In a heavy bottomed pot on medium-high heat, add remaining thyme and fennel seeds, garlic and 1 cup white wine. Simmer rapidly and reduce by half. Add cream and continue to simmer, reducing by half or to desired consistency. Add leek and garlic purée to sauce. Stir in and serve with strudel.

1 cup spinach, blanched and drained

1 tablespoon garlic, finely diced

2 tablespoons shallots

6 tablespoons walnut oil

4 sheets phyllo dough

1 tablespoon fennel seeds

2 tablespoons fresh thyme

2 cups assorted mushrooms (lobster, shiitake, portobello, chicken of the woods, etc.)

4 pieces feta cheese (sliced 1/4 inch thick, 4 inches long)

1/2 cup leeks, chopped

1 tablespoon garlic, sliced

1 1/2 cups vermouth

2 cups 36 percent cream

Japanese Oxtail Soup

**Kamei Royale Ocean
Japanese Restaurant**
1333 Johnston St.
Vancouver, BC
(604) 602-0005

Experience the finest Japanese cuisine at Kamei Royale Ocean. Located on Granville Island, this 200-seat waterfront restaurant looks over beautiful False Creek and downtown Vancouver. Authentic Japanese dishes as well as seasonal West Coast style dishes, are featured in the menu.

The featured recipe, Japanese Oxtail Soup, combines the traditional style of Japanese cooking with creative ingredients to produce a well-balanced flavor.

An open patio on the pier is available in the summer for those who would prefer a lunch, a light snack with wine or a full dinner by the sail boats. Private tatami rooms overlooking the ocean are ideal for corporate and personal occasions. Free parking is available.

Golden yellow soup balanced with gingery flavour and extra tender oxtail.

Cut oxtail in pieces at the joints, remove its fat and wash clean. In a pot deep enough to submerge the meat, add 10 liters water. Add oxtail, ginger, peanuts, garlic and bay leaves. Mix well and bring to a boil. Keep simmering on low heat for 4 hours. Constantly remove lard that forms at the top of the soup. Add soy sauce, sake, mirin, sugar and salt to soup and mix well. Simmer for 1 hour more until color becomes a clear yellow. Serve with desired amount of green onion, cilantro and grated ginger in bowls.

5 pounds oxtail

2 1/2 ounces fresh ginger

4 ounces fresh garlic

4 ounces fresh peanuts

5 pieces dry bay leaves

10 ounces soy sauce

4 ounces sake (rice wine)

6 ounces mirin
(sweet cooking sake)

1 teaspoon sugar

1/2 teaspoon salt

1/4 cup green onion,
chopped

1/4 cup fresh cilantro

1/8 cup fresh ginger, grated

10 liters water

Angel Hair Pasta with Prawns

IL
DUCATO
RISTORANTE
Il Ducato
2042 West Fourth Avenue
Vancouver, BC
(604) 739-7675

Il Ducato, nestled in the heart of trendy Kitsilano, is calming yet sophisticated. Mediterranean décor, with shell-pink ceiling arches and a warm, cozy fireplace, adds to the traditional warmth and romantic ambiance. Owners Natino Bellantoni and Mario Turco, along with Chef David Hossack, have created a cheerful Italian eatery where the staff is friendly and knowledgeable. Menu presentation with excellent descriptions and an award-winning wine list (Silver Medal from Vancouver Playhouse Wine Festival), clearly denote a variety in winery and appellation. All of which point to the hosts and chef, who realize that every detail counts. Dining at Il Ducato is completely satisfying, from the moment you walk in the door to when the hosts all say goodnight.

A melody of prawns, scallops and assorted herbs on a bed of angel hair pasta.

Cook pasta according to package directions. Drain and place in a warm serving bowl. Sprinkle with olive oil. Meanwhile, heat two tablespoons of oil in a large skillet and cook prawns and scallops until half done. Remove from heat. Add garlic, green onions, sun-dried tomatoes, roma tomatoes, half of white wine, half of olive oil. Sauté for two minutes. Return prawns and scallops to the skillet and add remaining olive oil, wine and lemon juice. Cook until prawns are done. Then add fresh herbs and toss. Mix together with pasta, salt and pepper to taste. Serve.

12 to 16 ounces mixed prawns (deveined) and scallops

8 to 10 ounces angel hair pasta (vermicellini)

1/4 cup extra virgin olive oil

1/4 cup dry white wine

1/2 cup fresh roma tomato

1/4 cup sun-dried tomatoes

1/2 cup green onion, sliced

3 cloves garlic, minced

3/4 cup fresh herbs, basil, dill, Italian parsley, thyme

2 tablespoons fresh lemon juice

Crispy Duck Breast

Located right in the heart of the city, Beetnix Restaurant features consistently fresh food, complemented by friendly service and a very affordable wine list. All served in a casually elegant setting. Chef Adrienne Woolfries offers award-winning entrées, including fresh duck, ahi tuna, meats, chicken, homemade gnocchi, pastas and her award-winning warm bread and tomato salad. Adrienne's featured recipe would be complemented perfectly with a fine Cabernet Sauvignon or Merlot. Reservations are recommended on weekends. Lunches served from Monday to Friday; dinners from Monday to Saturday; closed Sundays.

Beetnix

Beetnix
2549 Cambie Street
Vancouver, BC
(604) 874-7133

Breast of duck served with caramelized onion and brie soufflé and port-soaked fig sauce

Preheat oven to 400 degrees. Pour port over figs, allow to mascerate. Rub duck breasts with Dijon mustard, salt, pepper, meat side only. Marinate 2 hours. Sauté onions on medium heat until caramelized. Increase heat and add garlic and bourbon; stand back as bourbon will flame up. Cook until liquid has evaporated, season with salt, pepper; allow onions to cool. Whisk together cream, whole eggs, egg yolks, cayenne, salt and pepper. Grease 4 to 5 ounce ramekins. Evenly distribute onions in each ramekin, add brie to each. Fill with egg mixture, place in oven. After 10 minutes, heat large sauté pan over medium heat and lay breasts skin side down in pan. Cook for 15 minutes. Do not blacken. Breasts render their own fat as they cook, leaving skin crisp. Turn breasts over and allow to cook for 1 minute.

Sauté shallots over medium heat, add figs and reduce liquid by half. Add veal stock; reduce sauce until it coats the back of a spoon. Season with salt, pepper. Remove soufflé from oven when golden, run a sharp knife around edge of ramekin and gently bang on counter. Place soufflé in middle of plate. Slice each breast very thinly on bias, fanning breast out around soufflés. Spoon sauce over each breast and enjoy!

4 8 ounce duck breasts, fresh

2 tablespoons dijon mustard

1 cup onion, finely chopped

3 cloves garlic, minced

1/8 cup Jack Daniel bourbon

3 whole eggs, plus 2 egg yolks

3/4 cup whipping cream

1/4 teaspoon cayenne pepper

4 small pieces of brie (about the size of a cherry)

1 shallot, minced

1/4 cup black mission figs, stems removed and sliced

1/4 cup port

1 cup veal stock

salt and pepper to taste

Lamb Osso-Bucco

Tommy O's
2590 Commercial Drive
Vancouver, BC
(604) 874-3445

Commercial Drive's secret little jewel. A standout on a street of good solid Italian neighbourhood restaurants, Tommy O's is a twenty-year tradition that has become a Vancouver fixture. Relax in a warm and elegant setting where you are greeted with a friendly smile in true Italian fashion. The service is contagiously enthusiastic in an especially beautiful atmosphere. Imagine the mood of the evening as the candlelight bounces off the white marble table tops. A celebration of taste-tempting specialties include Smoked Black Alaskan Cod, Lamb Osso-Bucco and Conchiglie filled with Crab and Spinach and Ricotta Cheese, along with many combinations of pasta and sauces. A carefully chosen wine list complements the extensive menu. Tommy O's is truly a memorable dining experience.

Braised lamb in a tomato vegetable broth served with bowtie pasta

Heat a large saucepan with 1 1/2 tablespoons olive oil over moderate heat, but not to point of smoking. Put in two lamb shanks and cook both sides for 10 minutes until golden. In a roasting pot with 1 1/2 tablespoons of olive oil, put in onion, celery, carrots and bell peppers along with rosemary, garlic and basil. Cook the vegetables until golden. Then add white beans, plum tomatoes, black pepper, red wine, veal stock, salt and the lamb shanks. Bring to a boil and cook for 10 minutes. Preheat oven at 450 degrees and cover roasting pot with a lid or use aluminum foil. Cook for about 50 minutes. Then serve with bed of bowtie pasta, and sprinkle with fresh sage and garnish with tomato concasse.

2 large lamb shanks
(approximately 2 pounds)

1/4 cup each celery, carrots, red bell pepper and onion, diced

1/2 teaspoon ground black pepper

1/2 tablespoon garlic, minced

3 cups veal stock

1/2 cup Piñot Noir red wine

3/4 cup bowtie pasta, cooked

1 teaspoon each fresh rosemary, chopped basil

1 tablespoon tomato paste

3 tablespoons olive oil

3 tablespoons white beans

3 large plum tomatoes

1 1/2 teaspoons salt

1 teaspoon butter (for pasta)

1/2 teaspoon fresh sage

Mulvaney's Chaucha

Since 1975, Mulvaney's New Orleans cuisine has been delighting locals and visitors. Located next to the Granville Island Market, the restaurant overlooks beautiful False Creek. Its turn of the century decor features a unique ceiling adrift in billowing fabrics and luxurious lamp shades which create an ambiance that is relaxed and comfortable. Mulvaney's offers a full range menu with house classics such as Rack of Lamb Lafayette, Scallops and Prawns Etouffee, Jambalaya and the famous Cajun Cioppino (seasonal shellfish poached in white wine, tomatoes and fresh herbs).

Mulvaney's
1535 Johnston St.
Vancouver, BC
(604) 685-6571

Chicken and seafood in sun-dried tomato cream sauce

In a deep frying pan heat the olive oil. Add the chicken tenderloins and garlic. Sauté quickly by moving frequently with wooden spoon until browned evenly. Flame with bourbon, then add stock and bring to boil. Add the cream, herbs and sun-dried tomatoes. Simmer until the liquid starts to thicken. Add fish and cover. Cook for three minutes on low heat. Add scallops, prawns and seasoning. Cook until prawns turn colour. Serve in small individual casserole dishes with fresh vegetables and rice pilaf.

olive oil

4 ounces chicken tenders

4 ounces fresh assorted fish, 1 inch cubes

1 ounce bourbon

1/2 ounce sun-dried tomatoes, sliced

1 teaspoon fresh chopped herbs (basil, rosemary, thyme, parsley)

4 medium shiitake mushrooms, sliced

1 ounce stock (fish or chicken)

1/4 teaspoon chopped garlic

1 cup whipping cream

2 scallops

2 tiger prawns

salt and pepper to taste

Filettini alla Siciliana

La Mansione Ristorante

La Mansione Ristorante
46290 Yale Road
Chilliwack, BC
(604) 792-8910

La Mansione Ristorante opened in 1978 and is situated in a beautiful heritage house built in 1911 by the Ekert family of Chilliwack. Designed by well-known architect, Sam McLure, the home was originally called Stonehurst (Stone House). A focal point of the community, this culinary landmark steadily gains clientele from all over the Lower Mainland and south of the border. The continental menu is varied and reflects the unparalleled natural bounty of the Fraser Valley. An impressive array of fresh seafoods, veal, great steaks and unique pasta dishes allow the distinctive Italian heritage to come through. Your host and the owner of La Mansione is Peter Graham. Peter's goal is to make everyone feel at home while presenting a great dining experience. This is accomplished by serving up fine cuisine in a professional manner in an inviting, friendly atmosphere. Peter loves the country lifestyle as compared to the city, where he learned his craft in some of Vancouver's finest and busiest establishments. His philosophy is: "We've been to the market, picked out the foods with great care, now enjoy the company of family and friends, it's a gift you can share".

Tender medallions of beef seared in piquant Italian spice, flambé with brandy

Heat frying pan or skillet to medium-high heat. Add oil and heat. Place 2 pieces of tenderloin in skillet and dust lightly with partial amount of crushed peppercorns, chili flakes and seasoning salt. Turn steaks over when browned completely on one side. Remove steaks from pan; remove pan from heat. Put steaks in preheated oven (400 degrees) to finish cooking. Pour off any oil from frying pan. Put pan back on stove, add onions and sauté until golden brown. Add red wine and brandy (use caution, brandy may flambé). Add beef jus or gravy and add remaining peppercorns and chili flakes, stirring constantly until reduced (coats back of a spoon). Remove steaks from oven and drizzle peppercorn sauce over. Serve and Enjoy!

2 3 ounce beef tenderloin steaks

2 tablespoons peppercorns, crushed with meat tenderizer

1 tablespoons oil

1/2 teaspoon chili flakes

1 tablespoon white onion, diced

6 ounces quality beef jus or gravy

1/2 ounce brandy

seasoning salt to taste

1 ounce red wine

1 tablespoon green Madagascar peppercorns

Grilled Beef with Piri Piri Sauce

O'Doul's
1300 Robson Street
Vancouver, BC
(604) 661-1400

O'Doul's Restaurant and Bar is evocative of the days of discovery; a massive sepia-toned Old World twin-hemisphere map dominates the atrium ceiling, while compass roses hover above our 68-foot solid Honduran mahogany bar. From farther afield and from around the world, the finest of wines and spirits are offered at O'Doul's, where art and elegance converge. European-trained chefs explore and revel in the rich flavors and bountiful harvest of the abundant Pacific coast and the fertile Fraser Valley delta. On the weekends, experience live jazz featuring some of Vancouver's hottest artists. The flavor is international—the ambiance, always uniquely Vancouver.

Sizzling Prime Cut grilled with a zesty sauce.

Combine all sauce ingredients and bring to a boil in saucepan. Boil for 4 minutes on high heat. Remove from heat, add garlic (2 ounces minced). Cool and blend in a food processor while warm until completely blended. Store in refrigerator. Sambal Oleck chili paste can be added to boost heat of sauce. Once you have selected your cut of beef, marinade in small amount of Piri Piri sauce overnight. Grill on barbeque or countertop smokeless grill. Start at high heat to sear both sides. Reduce heat to medium and continue to desired doneness. For 1 inch thickness: medium-rare—7 minutes; medium—10 minutes; well-done—15 to 20 minutes. Serve on 425 degree platter with fresh chopped herbs.

Wine Recommendations: As a general rule, stick to full-bodied reds to match the flavor and texture of beef. The age of the wine also becomes an important consideration. Older, softer reds more evenly match the taste of well-aged cuts (Rib Eye, New York). Younger barrel-aged reds still have depth and complexity and match well with Tenderloin.

Steaks

Rib Eye—richly marbled, flavorful and tender

New York—connoisseur's choice, full-bodied flavor

Tenderloin—classic filet, the most tender cut

Piri Piri Sauce

1 liter olive oil

1 ounce dry thyme

1 ounce dry basil

1 ounce rosemary

3 bay leaves

1 teaspoon cracked chili peppers

1 teaspoon cracked black pepper

8 jalapeño peppers with seeds

1 tablespoon salt

Measurements & Equivalents

1 tablespoon
3 teaspoons
15 ml

1/4 cup
4 tablespoons
60 ml

1/2 cup
4 fl. ounces
100 ml

1 cup
8 fl. ounces
225 ml

2 cups
1 pint
475 ml

2 pints
1 quart
950 ml

5 grams
1 teaspoon

25 grams
1 ounce
2 tablespoons

100 grams
4 ounces
1/4 pound

225 grams
8 ounces
1/2 pound

450 grams
16 ounces
1 pound

1 kilogram
2.2 pounds
35 ounces

1 pound prawns
30 - 40 medium prawns
25 - 30 jumbo prawns

1 serving salmon
5 ounces
150 grams

1 stick of butter
1/4 pound
1/2 cup

juice of 1 lemon
3 tablespoons lemon juice
45 ml lemon juice

2 eggs
4 egg yolks
1/4 cup

1 cup raw rice
2 - 3 cups cooked

Substitutions

1 ounce bittersweet chocolate

use 3 tablespoons cocoa plus
1 1/2 teaspoon fat or 1 tablespoon
liquid Butter Buds

1 cup cake flour

1 cup minus 1 tablespoon
all-purpose flour

1 teaspoon dry mustard

1 tablespoon prepared mustard

1 teaspoon baking powder

1/4 teaspoon baking soda plus 1/2 cup
buttermilk or sour milk (to replace
1/2 cup of the liquid in the recipe)

2 cups tomato sauce

use 3/4 cup tomato paste
plus 1 cup water

1 cup self-rising flour

1 cup all-purpose flour, 1/2 teaspoon
baking soda, 1 1/2 teaspoons baking
powder, and 1/2 teaspoon light salt

1 package active dry yeast

1 cake compressed yeast

1 tablespoon cornstarch

(for thickening)

2 tablespoons all-purpose flour

1 clove garlic

1/8 teaspoon garlic powder or
1/8 teaspoon minced dried garlic or
1/2 teaspoon minced garlic in a jar

oil

use applesauce, cup for cup

chicken broth

use honey, cup for cup

1 small onion

1 teaspoon onion powder
or tablespoon minced dried
onion, rehydrated

1 teaspoon grated lemon peel

1/2 teaspoon lemon extract

1 cup white sugar

1 cup brown sugar or 2 cups sifted
powdered sugar or 1 cup molasses
plus 1/4 to 1/2 teaspoon baking soda.
Reduce liquid by 1/4 cup

1 cup buttermilk

1 tablespoon lemon juice or vinegar
plus skim milk to make 1 cup

Wine Suggestions

Light & Delicate White-
Sauvignon Blanc
Seafood, Shellfish, Fish

Fuller Bodied White-
Chardonnay, Pinot Blanc
Chicken, Veal, Pork, Fish with
Tomatoes, Heavier Poultry

Light-Bodied Red-
Pinot Noir
Lamb, Beef, Stews

Full-Bodied Red-
Cabernet, Merlot
Game, Mediterranean Food

Rose-
White Zinfandel
Seafood, Fish, Chicken, Veal, Pork,
Poultry, Game, Mediterranean Food

Sweet Dessert Wine-
Johannisberg Riesling,
late harvest Mucat
Desserts

Herb Chart

Allspice-
Meatball appetizers, beef stew, pot roast, ham, lamb, oysters

Basil-
Turtle soup, meat loaf, venison, halibut, goose, duck, turkey

Bay Leaf-
Beef stew, fish chowders, spareribs, shrimp, crab, seafood casseroles

Cloves-
Beef soup, ham, pork roasts, baked fish, roasted chicken

Curry Powder-
Clam chowder, chicken soup, lamb, veal, shrimp, baked fish

Garlic-
Barbecue sauce, steaks, stews, Italian & French meat dishes, chicken, fish

Ginger-
Boiled beef, lamb, veal, baked or sauteed chicken, cornish hen

Marjoram-
Pot roast, stews, lamb, scallops, broiled fish

Mustard-
Meat dips, ham sauces, beef-onion soup, lamb

Nutmeg-
Cream of chicken soup, salisbury steak, meat loaf, chicken

Oregano-
Meat sauces, beef, pork, veal, lamb, Swiss steak, fried chicken

Paprika-
Egg dishes, chicken, potato salad, stews, goulash

Rosemary-
Chicken or meat soups, veal stews, lamb, creamed shellfish

Saffron-
Poultry stuffing, chicken soup stock, lamb, veal, sausage, chicken, halibut

Sage-
Meat sauces and gravies, chowders, cold roast beef, stews, pork dishes

Tarragon-
Meat sauces, meat canape mixtures, veal, sweet breads, turkey, game, chicken, chicken salads

Thyme-
Meat sauces, chowders, oyster stew

Glossary

Anchovies-

Small, silvery saltwater fish that come from the Mediterranean and the coastlines of southern Europe. They are usually filleted, salted and canned in oil. To alleviate saltiness, soak in water for 30 minutes, drain and pat dry with paper towel.

Beans-

Beans can be broken down into two categories - fresh and dried. The three most common fresh bean varieties are green beans, lima beans and fava beans. Popular dried beans include black beans, chickpeas, kidney beans and white beans. Dried beans must usually be soaked in water before cooking.

Bell Peppers-

They have a mild, sweet taste and crisp, juicy flesh. Most are deep green in color and are available year-round. Other varieties are seasonal and include yellow, red, orange, brown and purple.

Butter-

Butter may be salted or unsalted. For best cooking results, use unsalted. Butter quickly absorbs flavor, so it should be wrapped airtight for storage.

Capers-

Capers are small buds of a bush common to the Mediterranean. The buds are sun-dried and pickled in a vinegar brine. They can be found packed in brine or salted and sold in bulk. Rinse before using to remove excess salt.

Chile Peppers-

Chiles come in more than 200 varieties. They vary from mild to extremely hot in taste and vary in coloring. For best cooking results, choose chiles with deep, vivid colors. Wear rubber gloves when preparing to avoid burning of the eyes. If no gloves are used, be sure to wash hands thoroughly after preparation.

Cornstarch-

Generally used as a thickening agent in a variety of foods. You may want to mix it with a small amount of cold liquid or a granular solid before stirring it in with a hot mixture. This will help prevent the formation of lumps.

Eggs-

Large eggs should be used when preparing the recipes in this book. The color of the eggshell does not affect the taste or nutritional value. Always refrigerate. For best flavor and quality, use eggs within one week.

Flours-

All-purpose flour is most commonly used for baking. Its two basic forms are bleached and unbleached. Bleached flour produces a tender result whereas unbleached more crisp. Flour greased baking pans to help remove goods more easily.

Mushrooms-

There are thousands of varieties of mushrooms. The cultivated white mushroom has a mild, earthy flavor and is readily available. Other varieties include the shiitake, morel, puffball and portobello. Store fresh mushrooms with cool air circulating around them. When using them whole, use mushrooms of

equal size to ensure even cooking. Before using, wipe with a damp paper towel or rinse them with cold water and dry thoroughly.

Mustard, Dijon-

A pale, grayish-yellowish mustard originally made in Dijon, France. It is made from brown or black mustard seeds, white wine or wine vinegar, unfermented grape juice and various seasonings. Its flavor ranges from mild to hot.

Nuts-

Any of a variety of dry fruits that are rich and mellow in flavor. Some popular nuts include almonds, cashews, chestnuts, macadamias, pecans, peanuts, pistachios, pine nuts and walnuts. When possible, buy nuts that are plump, crisp and uniform in size and color. Nuts should always be purchased and used as fresh as possible for best flavor. Store them in an airtight container in a cool place.

Oils-

Oils are used for cooking, baking and enhancing the texture and flavor of foods. Oils generally come from vegetable sources. Varieties include almond, olive, extra virgin olive, light olive, coconut, canola, safflower, corn and peanut. Most oils should be stored in a cool, dark place.

Olives-

Small, oily fruit native to the Mediterranean area. There are many varieties that vary in size and color. Black olives are cured in brine or salt and are generally packed in olive oil or vinegar. You may store unopened olives for up to two years at room temperature.

Glossary

Onions-

The two main categories of onions are green and dry. Green onions, also known as scallions, have a sweet, mild flavor because they have a high water and sugar content. Dry onions have a juicy flesh covered with multiple layers of dry skin. All varieties of onions may be braised, boiled, steamed, baked, sautéed, scalloped, fried or grilled. Sauté onions to soften their texture and enrich their taste. Also, you may want to simmer onions in wine or broth instead of butter in order to lower the fat content. Freeze the onion for 20 minutes before you are prepared to chop them to alleviate any tearing of the eyes.

Pastas-

A wide variety of noodles made from an Italian type of dough that is semolina combined with water or milk. Pasta that is made with flour and eggs is generally referred to as noodles. Spaghetti and macaroni are two of the most popular of the varieties. Conchiglie is shell-shaped; farfalle is bow-shaped; and rotelle is shaped like little corkscrews. Ravioli and tortellini have fillings, often meat and cheese. Green pasta is colored with spinach; red with tomato or beet juice; and squid ink is used to create charcoal gray. Fresh pasta cooks faster than dried, but is highly perishable. Use light sauces for delicate pastas and heavy sauces for sturdy pastas.

Shellfish-

Shellfish include a variety of underwater creatures. Be sure that all lobsters are alive when you purchase them. Lobster is best when it is broiled or boiled. Shrimp comes in a variety of colors including shades of red, brown, yellow, gray and green. Texture and flavor does not vary much among shrimp. Boil, fry or grill them for the best flavor. Crab meat is sweet and succulent and is best when fried, boiled, steamed or used in a dish. Mussels have a sweet flavored meat and are best when steamed, fried or baked. There are two types of scallops - bay and sea. It is best to cook them for a short period of time. Scallops may be sautéed, grilled, broiled or poached. They are often used in a variety of salads, stews and soups.

Soy Sauce-

A dark, salty sauce made from soy beans, wheat, salt and water and is a main ingredient in Asian cooking. It has a shelf life of many months when stored in a cool, dark place. It is used to flavor a variety of foods and is often a tasty table condiment.

Spices-

Sweet or savory seasonings obtained from the bark, dried seeds, roots, fruit, buds or stems of a variety of plants and trees. Spices should always be used sparingly. Allspice is brown in color and may be purchased either ground or whole. It is used for all types of cooking. Cardamom is a member of the ginger family. It has a strong aroma, with a warm, sweet flavor. It can be used to flavor dishes such as stews and curries. Ceylon cinnamon is mildly sweet, whereas cassia (the most common cinnamon) has a strong, slightly bittersweet taste. It is commonly used as a flavoring for cooking sweet dishes. Cloves can be used to flavor with a touch of sweetness and has a strong, spicy aroma. Mace is used to flavor all different kinds of foods. Nutmeg has a warm, sweet and spicy flavor. It is a delicious additive used in baked goods, milk-based foods, fruits and vegetables. Paprika is a seasoning used in savory dishes. Its flavor ranges from mild to hot.

Pepper is the most common spice. The peppercorn comes in three varieties - black, white and green. Saffron is a golden-orange spice and is mainly used to flavor and tint food.

Sugars-

There are many types of sugars used to sweeten various recipes. Sugar not only sweetens, it can also make dough tender, add stability to mixtures, brown the surfaces of baked goods and help preserve foods. Granulated (white) sugar is the most common sugar used for cooking. It is highly refined and made from beets or cane. Confectioners' sugar is finely pulverized with a small amount of cornstarch added to prevent clumping. It is also used to make icings, candy and decorative coatings on desserts. Brown sugar, light or dark, is white sugar that has been combined with molasses. It tastes rich and has a soft texture. The darker the brown, the more molasses flavoring.

Tomatoes-

There are dozens of tomato varieties available, but for cooking, beefsteak and plum tomatoes are the best. Beefsteak tomatoes have a delicious bright red, slightly elliptical-shape and are good for eating raw or for cooking. Plum tomatoes are egg-shaped and are red or yellow in color, and can be purchased canned for cooking. When selecting, choose firm, well-shaped tomatoes that smell good and have a deep color. The perfect tomato should have no blemishes, be heavy for its size and give slightly when pressed in the palm of your hand. Store ripe tomatoes at room temperature and use them as quickly as possible. They last only a few days. Never refrigerate. Cold temperatures make them lose flavor and develop a pulpy flesh.

Restaurant Index

Recipe Index

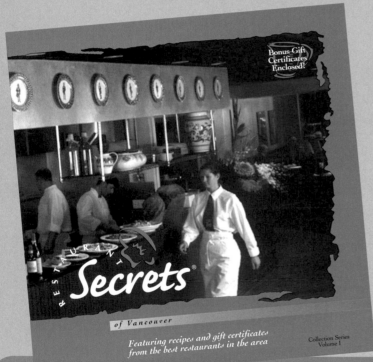